"ONE OF THE MOST TROUBLESOME ROBBERY GANGS"

The Murders and Crimes of George McKeever and Francis McNeiley

Jeffery S. King

ISBN: 978-1-7349573-0-3 (Paperback)
ISBN: 978-1-7349573-1-0 (Ebook)

Washington, D.C., Frank Manley Publishing Company, 2020

ACKNOWLEDGEMENTS

Damia Torhagen did an excellent job of editing. I thank the Historical Societies of Minnesota and Missouri for providing me with photographs. Many local libraries gave me newspaper articles. Ingrid Hidalgo provided computer service.

TABLE OF CONTENTS

INTRODUCTION

The Missouri Highway Patrol, consisting of a superintendent appointed by the Governor, ten captains and 114 patrolmen, came to be in 1931.[1] It was soon put to the test, when Missouri suffered three catastrophic events; the "Young Brothers Massacre" (January 2, 1932),[2] the "Crossroads murders" (June 14, 1933),[3] and the "Kansas City Massacre" (June 17, 1933).[4]

At the "Young Brothers Massacre" six police officers were killed by two brothers near Springfield, Missouri, the worst police massacre in United States history. So many police lives were lost because there was no training and planning by the police, who did not have powerful weapons.[5]

At the "Crossroads Murders" two lawmen were murdered near Columbia, Missouri, at a roadblock by bank robbers George McKeever and Francis McNeiley, not captured for over a year.[6]

At the "Kansas City Massacre" three officers, an FBI agent, and criminal Frank Nash were killed by Pretty Boy Floyd, Adam Richetti and Verne Miller at the Kansas City, Missouri, Union Station. The lawmen were attempting to take Nash to Leavenworth Prison from the Union Station.[7] During this period J. Edgar Hoover and the Federal Bureau of Investigation became very powerful. Before July 1935 the FBI was known as the Bureau of Investigation or the

Division of Investigation. The so-called "war on crime" began at the time of the massacre.[8]

There followed the sensational captures and killings of major criminals who became famous mostly by the FBI: Machine Gun Kelly on September 26, 1933; Clyde Barrow and Bonnie Parker on May 23, 1934: John Dillinger on July 22, 1934; Pretty Boy Floyd on October 22, 1934; Baby Face Nelson (an alias of Lester Joseph Gillis) November 27, 1934; Ma Barker and her son Fred on January 16, 1935, and Alvin Karpis on May 1, 1936.[9]

The Roaring Twenties was a period of economic prosperity and major social change in the United States. For the first time, more people lived in urban areas. By the mid-twenties, prosperity was widespread. The period saw the common use of automobiles, airplanes, telephones, radios, movies and electricity. Big changes occurred in culture, such as the advancement of women, who, finally won the right to vote.

1920 saw a Prohibition amendment added to the United States Constitution; that made illegal the manufacture, import, and sale of beer, wine and hard liquor. Prohibition was enacted through the Volstead Act, which up opened American to the rise of organized crime. Al Capone of Chicago was the most famous gangster of the era. Speakeasies, where someone could buy a homemade, illegal drink, became popular and common, had strong connections to organized crime, and lured people in with luxury food, live bands, and floor shows. Police were bribed to pretend they did not exist.[10]

The world-wide Great Depression, damned the Roaring Twenties to a sudden halt on September 4, 1929, when stock prices began to free-fall. The stock market fully crashed on October 29, 1929. Personal income, profits, prices and tax revenue dropped; and international trade fell by more than 50% overnight. Unemployment sky-rocketed 25%. At "soup kitchens" people stood in long lines to get food at. Some depressed businessmen jumped to their deaths from tall buildings. Many became homeless hobos living in shantytowns.

Cities with major heavy industry severely suffered. There was little construction. Areas with mining and logging industries were badly hit. Farmers and rural people were big losers, as crop prices fell about 60%. Many lost their farm. Several years of drought and erosion led to the Dust Bowl in the Mid-west; few crops could be grown there. Many thousands of farmers and the unemployed went to California to find work.[11]

During the Great Depression, law enforcement was weak. Criminals, had the advantage; faster cars and better weapons. The few poorly-trained lawmen were constrained to their county or state borders. Police radios were rare. The FBI in the early 1930s had only 266 agents, all with little authority. The *Tulsa* OK *Daily World* asked for a "Highway Patrol" like the new Missouri Highway Patrol, which it thought would be effective against bank robbers because they would be well-trained and could operate all over Missouri. In many towns vigilantes were organized.[12]

It became obvious Law enforcement reform was necessary. Little coordination and cooperation existed among federal, state, county or municipal police forces. State police were very small, often only patrolling state highways. Bribe taking County and city police sometimes even protected criminals. Police brutality was widespread. In America scientific police work was very limited. While fingerprinting was replacing the ineffective Bertillon method of criminal identification by physical measurements, police and courts had little use for scientific methods.[13]

The first use of ballistic forensics was from 1835 to 1888, when there were simple observation, experiments, physical traits matching and other determinations from the inspection of the size and shape of a projectile. From 1900 to 1930, forensic ballistics was recognized by U. S. courts and throughout the world. Several lawmen and scientists did intensive research and experiments to identify bullets and guns with specific firearms and bullets. In the United States, the Scientific Crime Detection Laboratory (SCDL) began operations at Northwestern University in 1930. Two years later, the Federal Bureau of Investigation Laboratory was created. In 1935 the Missouri Scientific Crime Detection Laboratory was established. Ballistics and fingerprint evidence were very important in the investigations of the three massacres.[14]

Many believed that only the federal government could help everyday citizens. Nevertheless, it was generally thought that the federal government should not fight most crime because it would became too powerful. Supposedly, this was forbidden by the U S Constitution and by states' rights, and only state and local governments could battle major crime.

Federal law enforcement power gained a significant boost in 1932 with the enactment of federal kidnapping statutes, spurred by the kidnapping and murder of the young son of aviator hero Charles Lindbergh. Nevertheless, President Herbert Hoover's attorney general, William D. Mitchell, still told Congress, "You are never going to correct the crime situation in this country by having Washington jump in."[15]

In 1932, the election of Franklin Delano Roosevelt for President made change in law enforcement power possible. He believed the federal government could deal with the serious economic and social conditions, even the crime wave of the Great Depression era. After he took office, he ended Prohibition in December 1933. Big-time bootleggers went out of business, but then turned to robbing banks and kidnapping rich people. Situations worsened instead of getting better.[16]

The American people did not want a "Secret Police." Director of the Bureau of Investigation, J. Edgar Hoover, and U. S. Attorney General, Homer S. Cummings, wanted to promote the idea that only the Federal government could handle the crime wave successfully. Both worked for new federal crime laws and increased law enforcement powers, unlike William ·Mitchell.[17]

McKeever and McNeiley were active criminals during the Great Depression and, surprisingly, "alter egos" of gangsters Pretty Boy Floyd and Adam Richetti. McKeever was mistaken for Floyd, Richetti for McNeiley. This "contributed almost as much to the legends built up around the Southwest's 'phantom killer {Floyd}.'" McKeever was sometimes called "Pretty Boy Floyd No. 2." Lawmen thought Floyd had a d ouble, his "alter ego." Often Floyd was reported to be in different places at the same time. Since these reports were found to be false and there were no credible sightings of Floyd at the time, many officers believed the outlaw must be dead, "the legend living after him."[18]

McKeever and McNeiley were almost the same size as Floyd and Richetti; both about five feet seven inches tall and 135 pounds. Four years older than Floyd, McKeever had a swarthy complexion, with very dark hair, black eyes, and a tattoo of a snake and dagger on his right forearm. He had another tattoo of an Indian chief standing near a rock on his left forearm. McNeiley, two years older than Richetti, had dark brown hair and blue gray eyes.[19]

Charles Arthur Floyd was about five feet 8 inches tall, weighed 155 pounds, had dark hair, gray eyes, a medium complexion, and was chunky with strong shoulders. The gangster had a tattoo of a nurse in a rose on his left forearm and four gold caps on his upper front teeth.[11][20]

McKeever and McNeiley did not became nationally famous, or even well-known, in some regions, because the FBI never showed interest in them. They were captured by local police and were not killed in a "blaze of glory." Nevertheless, the two gangsters were dangerous men, who robbed several banks in the Mid-west of at least $40,000 and killed two Missouri police officers and a Minnesota store owner. Today, that $40,000 would be worth almost $700,000. They also robbed stores, committed many burglaries, and stole cars. Like famous criminal "alter egos" of the time they long eluded police. McNeiley and two others escaped from two Iowa lawmen in a sensational car chase and machine-gun battle, which received national headlines.[21] Most of the famous lone-wolf criminals of the time stole and killed more than McKeever and McNeiley, but Bonnie and Clyde may have stolen less. Their big-gest robbery was only for $1,500. Floyd may have stolen less than $25,000. Machine Gun Kelly killed no one.[22]

PART ONE

CHAPTER 1

THE CROSSROADS MURDERS

At 2:15 PM, June 14, 1933, two short, slender men exited from a large blue sedan in front of the Farmers and Merchants' Bank of Mexico, Missouri, ready to rob it. Inside, were three men; cashier, C. F. Merrifield, and depositors, Ben B. Dobyns and Robert Lyon. The oldest of the two bandits, about 35-years-old, had light hair and gray eyes. He entered the bank, and pulled out an automatic pistol from his right coat pocket.

"Get 'em up—this is a stickup!" he yelled, and took about $85 from a customer trying to make a deposit.

The younger bandit, with dark hair and a sallow face, went behind the counter, grabbed $1,700 in cash and put it into a brown paper grocery bag he carried.

"If you move within five minutes, you'll get a dose of lead," the older bandit snarled.

They then fled to the getaway car, driven by a man in his thirties. Fifteen minutes later, a broadcast over the Missouri Highway Patrol radio in Jefferson City described the three criminals and the getaway car. The men were travelling south on U.S. 54, toward the intersection of U.S. 54 and U.S. 40, that linked St. Louis and Kansas City.[1]

It was a nice summer day in Columbia, Missouri. Missouri Highway Patrol Sergeant Ben Booth called Sheriff Roger Wilson, and asked for his help in capturing the bank robbers. Two days before, Wilson, a Freemason, had celebrated his 43rd birthday. It was just in January that the sheriff was sworn in. He was married, with one child.[2] Born on June 20, 1890, in Cedar, Missouri; his parents were William, a farmer, and Ophelia Wilson.[3]

Booth was born in 1894 in Missouri, to John W. and Alice Booth. The 39-year-old patrolman served overseas during World War 1. Afterwards, he was a laborer on his father's farm for several years before joining the Columbia police force. Married, with two children, Booth had been a patrolman since the beginning of the Missouri Highway Patrol in 1931.[4]

Around 3:15 P.M., at the highway intersection, just north of Columbia in the village of Kingdom City, the lawmen set up a roadblock to catch the robbers. A few minutes later, two gangsters not involved in the bank robbery, George McKeever and Francis McNeiley, drove up to the roadblock. Several people witnessed the gunfight that followed.

Holding out his hand in a stop gesture, Sergeant Booth stepped into the road to block the oncoming vehicle. He went to the driver's side of the car, asked McNeiley for his name, where he was going, and his address. Booth saw many guns in the car; and, then, went around to the passenger side window, reached inside, and opened the car door.

"Get out," he yelled.

McKeever fired a Colt .45 semi-automatic pistol, hitting Booth's left leg. The bullet went downward, deflected at the knee, and stuck in his left ankle. Still, in front of the Ford, Sheriff Wilson drew his gun and fired; McNeiley fired two shots from a .38-caliber revolver, hitting the sheriff twice in the head, killing him instantly. Wilson's hat flew off. One bullet buried itself behind his right ear. Another one went through the left side of his head, going slightly upward, clipping the left ear, as it exited his body, with his skull fractured two-thirds of the way around.

Meanwhile, the wounded Sergeant pulled McKeever from the car. Booth desperately tried to get the pistol. McNeiley left the vehicle, and shot the sergeant thorough the back at the seventh rib. The bullet nicked the spine, and finally rested in the left shoulder. As Booth fell and lay still on the ground, McKeever attempted to shoot Booth again, but the .45 jammed.

"You didn't kill him," McKeever screamed as he grabbed the .38 from McNeiley, and fired at Booth's heart. The bullet entered the left nipple and the left chest cavity, then penetrated the tip of the left lung, gouging a track through the heart. After crossing the right chest cavity into the right lung, it exited the body.

After brushing his hair and dusting off his clothes, McKeever leapt into his vehicle. His partner joined him, and they headed east. As the gangsters passed a nearby gas station, its owner fired two errant rifle shots at them. Booth, the first Missouri highway patrolman to be killed in the line of duty, died on the way to the hospital.[5]

The killers fled east on Route 40, and stopped twelve miles away at Englewood, Missouri.

There they got gas, which they did not pay for, and went on to Fulton, Missouri.[6] About 9:30 P.M., the gangsters drove up to the Standard Oil Company station at Shelbina, Missouri. Station manager, Harry Turney, wiped off the windshield, and filled the gas tank. The gangsters asked for a small can of oil and entered the station office. As Turney leaned over to get the oil can, they pointed a gun at him, and stole about $10. When Turney's son, Harry, Jr., came into the station, the robbers forced he and his father to go into the restroom, and locked them in. The robbers then left.[7]

Later, the criminals bought sandwiches and soda pop in Edina, Missouri. They continued through northern Missouri, entered

Iowa, crossed into Illinois and reached St. Louis mid-afternoon on the 15th. That night and the next day, the killers stayed in Mrs. Dorothy Schubert's boarding house. She had known McNeiley for about five years. On the 17th, they travelled to Pleasantville, Iowa, burned their car, and, then, on June 22, went to McKeever's mother's home in Burlington, Iowa. There, they met McKeever's brother, Eloy, and his wife, Anne, who was also McNeiley's sister. The murderers complained of having sore feet, the result of hitch-hiking from Pleasantville.[8]

CHAPTER 2

"LET US HOPE THAT THE HUNT WILL GO ON RELENTLESSLY"

News of the murders quickly spread by telegraph and radio. Some of witnesses said they saw three men, and others two. Roadblocks went up all over Missouri. The State offered a princely reward of $2,300 for the two killers. National Guard airplanes with their two-way communication with the radio station, WOS, joined the manhunt. Lawmen had to shoot at any cars not stopping at roadblocks. Huge posses of angry lawmen, National Guardsmen, and farmers hunted for the killers of the very popular officers. The next morning the *Columbia* Mo *Daily Tribune* reported that, if the murderers were caught, "their being brought to the police station alive was very unlikely."[1]

Pretty Boy Floyd and Adam Richetti took the blame for the murders. The two were known to be in the area, and there were eyewitness accounts identifying them. Floyd also was reported to have killed hapless victims, and, like Floyd, one of the killers was seen to be primping just after the killings.[2]

Led by Missouri Highway Patrol Captain, Lewis Means, the search in central Missouri was one of the most intense manhunts in the history of the state. Means had lived at Fayette, Missouri, most of his adult life. Signal honors for his military service accrued to him. A son of Andrew and Rebecca Means, he was born July 15, 1890, and reared on a farm near Greenfield, Missouri: here he attended high school before going to Fayette to attend Central College. He was a member of the 1910 championship football team, Central's first, and a member of the Aristotelain Literary Society. For several years, he was employed by the Cheoweth Clothing Company.

Upon the outbreak of World War I, Means enlisted in the National Guard, and, on August 15, 1917, he was commissioned an Second Lieutenant in an infantry division. At the end of the war, he commanded a company as a First Lieutenant. He returned to Fayette as a businessman during the 1920s. In 1922, he organized a National Guard infantry company in Fayette, and, soon, was promoted to Major.

When the Missouri Highway Patrol was created in 1931, Means was the first non-political appointee. As Executive Officer, he was in charge of the training and operations of the various troops.[3]

Large crowds at the Columbia police station headquarters, as well as in other Missouri towns, heard frequent radio messages from posses of officers and citizens, but there were few facts except the direction the getaway car went. No one seemed to have described the murders the same way. Governor Guy B. Park offered a "dead or alive" reward of $200. Boone County, Missouri, added another $200, and the city of Columbia added $100, for a total of $500.

On the night of the murders, Dr. C. C. Pflaum, Assistant Pathologist at the University of Missouri Medical School, performed autopsies on the slain officers. The next morning, Coroner E. G. Davis held an inquest in the police court room of the Fire and Police Building. A jury of six men viewed the bodies and heard the testimony of four eyewitnesses, who were interrogated by prosecution Attorney W. H. Sapp, Coroner Davis, and jury members. Dr. Pflaum testified that the wounds were responsible for the deaths of Sheriff Wilson and Sergeant Booth, and that the sheriff's skull was fractured two-thirds of the way around, the most trouble fracture of a skull he had ever seen. The coroner's jury returned a verdict that Sheriff Wilson and Sergeant Booth came to their deaths by gunshot wounds inflicted by unknown persons.[4]

The two killers were believed to be hiding in a f ive-square mile area of rugged hills, small Streams, and heavy underbrush in southern Callaway County, Missouri. After two sleepless nights, the search was abandoned at noon on June 16 by two hundred patrolmen, posse men, and National Guardsmen. Two National Guard companies were demobilized, and two National Guard airplanes returned to St. Louis. Governor Park and Director of the Missouri National Guard, Colonel B. Marvin Casteel, ordered the men "to get some rest."

Missouri City and County offices were closed that day in honor of the murdered men. Two thousand people, including state policemen, Columbia policemen, National Guardsmen and policemen from other cities, paid tribute to the dead officers. A large crowd visited the Willet Funeral Home before the courthouse services. Judge W. M. Dinwiddle presided, and Dr. C. C. Lemmon gave the invocation. Viewing of the two bodies was held at the Columbia courthouse from 10 A.M. to 1 P.M..

At 2:30 P.M., hundreds of family members and friends of Roger Wilson went to his burial. at the Nashville Church, ten miles away, with the Rev. Henry Cheavens officiating. During Cheavens's address, he paid the highest tribute to the two officers.[5]

Funeral service for Ben Booth was at the First Christian Church of Columbia on Saturday, June 1. At 10 A.M., 2000 people paid tribute to the dead officer at his burial at Memorial Park Cemetery in Columbia. State police officers served as pallbearers and honor guards. Led by Missouri National Guard Captain Lewis Means, a salute was fired over the grave and taps was Blown, as they lowered Booth's body into his grave. Dr. C. C. Lemmon gave the eulogy.[6]

On June 19, the *St. Louis Post-Dispatch* published an editorial entitled, "When Murderers Go Free." It warned officers that procrastination is to the advantage of the killers, and it expressed hope that the officers in that section and elsewhere would make the capture and conviction of the slayers a matter of "unfinished business."

According to the editorial:
The hunt for the murderers of Sheriff Wilson of Boone county and Sergeant Booth of the State Highway Patrol at Columbia Wednesday should be pressed with vigor until the murderers are captured and brought to trial. If they should escape and evade arrest for a few months, the task of prosecuting and convicting would be difficult. Delay and the technicalities of the law work wonderfully and fearfully to the criminal's advantage...

Certainly if...gangsters can kill a constable...and never be brought to trial, notwithstanding almost conclusive circumstantial evidence, that fact is an encouragement to professional criminals everywhere to shoot down officers as Sheriff Wilson and Sergeant Booth were shot down. When mail truck robbers can literally get away with murder...why should bank robbers hesitate to kill? After all, the statutes are the mere body of the law. The soul, the power, the majesty of the law abide in the purpose and character of officials charged with the enforcement of the law and the administration of justice. When prosecuting attorneys and courts stand helpless over the grave of murdered officers, then justice indeed is derided and the criminal is practically licensed to kill.

Let us hope the murder of Sheriff Wilson and Sergeant Booth will not be carried in any file as "unfinished business." Let us hope that the hunt will go on relentlessly until the murderers are caught, tried, convicted, and hanged.[7]

CHAPTER 3

THE KANSAS CITY MASSACRE

Saturday, June 17, 1933, dawned a bright morning, with the temperature a pleasant 71 degrees. It was only three days after McKeever and McNeiley had killed two Missouri lawmen. Pretty Boy Floyd, Verne Miller, and Adam Richetti parked at the front doors of the Kansas City Union Station. It bustled with the usual station noise: heel clicks on the marble floors, train arrival announcements, cab starters' whistles, and cabs and cars going by. Nearby was the popular Fred Harvey Restaurant.

The Little Rock Flyer arrived at 7:15 AM. On board were FBI agents, Frank Smith and Joe Lackey, along with McAlester, Oklahoma, Chief of Police, Otto Reed, and prisoner, Frank Nash. They got off the train and headed toward the stairwell that led to the station lobby. At the top of the stairs were two honest officers of the very corrupt Kansas City Police, thirteen year veteran, Frank Hermanson, and W. J. "Red" Grooms, a rookie police officer of only one year. With them were two Kansas City FBI office agents, Raymond J. Caffrey, and Kansas City Special Agent in Charge (SAC), R. E. Vetterli.

About 7:20 AM Nash's fan-shaped escort of seven lawmen walked through the station. Nash was in the middle of the group, his handcuffs barely covered by a handkerchief. Reed carried a sawed-off shotgun and a .38 revolver. Lackey also had a sawed-off shotgun, while the others had pistols. One officer kept his hand on his hip, so that he could draw his revolver quickly.

The officers left the station and crossed the plaza toward Caffrey's two-door Chevrolet that they planned to take to avoid the attention of an official car. Four agents and Chief Reed were to drive Nash to Leavenworth in the unmarked car; Hermanson and Grooms were to follow in another vehicle.

Gangsters Miller and Richetti were only 25 feet away hanging out on the running board of a car, and gangster Floyd was behind a lamppost, waiting for the lawmen and Nash to get to their cars, and then free Nash. After Caffrey unlocked the Chevy's right door, Nash started to climb into the back, but Caffrey told him to sit in the front seat. Lackey, Reed, and Smith quickly got into the back, with Smith in the middle. Grooms and Hermanson stood, with Vetterli near the right side of the hood.[1]

Quickly, Floyd moved from the lamppost behind the lawmen. He waved his machine gun and shouted, "Put 'em Up! Up! Up!"[2]

Miller and Richetti came out from behind a car. Then the unthinkable happened. Grooms drew his pistol and fired two shots at Floyd. Hopeless for the four men inside, Caffrey's car's windshield shattered from the gunfire. During the next ten seconds, Nash, Reed, Caffrey, Grooms, and Hermanson perished. Lackey and Vetterli took wounds. Only Smith was unhurt.[3]

Because he did not know how to use a shotgun, Lackey may have accidentally caused the deaths of Nash, Caffrey, Hermanson, and even Chief Reed.[4]

They all fired about one hundred shots. Bullets pockmarked the Union Station's walls. People fled in all directions. Cars crashed into other cars. Two Catholic nuns were paralyzed with fear. A redcap pushed a man in a wheelchair away at crazy speed.

"My God, is this Chicago?" someone cried out.[5]

Floyd and Miller looked inside Caffrey's bullet-ridden car.

"He's dead. They're all dead," Floyd yelled.[6]

Vetterli made a break for the station to put in a call for help. He got a flesh wound in his left arm for his trouble. As he ran, shots flew by his head and lodged in the Union Station bricks.

Motorcycle policeman, Mike Fanning, fired three shots. Floyd was hit in his left shoulder, while Miller took a slight wound in his right little finger.[7] With Miller at the wheel, the three murderers quickly made their escape, just missing a trolley car, as the gangsters ran a red light.[8]

Newspapers called the massacre a "Machine Gun Challenge to the Nation."[9] At the time, it was the second largest massacre of lawmen in American history, after the recent Young Brothers Massacre. Amazingly and tragically, in only one year and in one state, a dozen lawmen had been killed, including the two officers murdered in the crossroad murders, in Missouri.[10]

"That one's alive! He's alive."[11]

When the first people ran up to the crime scene, gun smoke was still hung over the Union Station parking lot. Ray Caffrey's body lay on the ground, his eyes open, his jaw moving, but he soon would be dead. Nearby the two dead Kansas City detectives lay in a welter of blood. Red Groom's body was on Hermanson's chest. With his head back, his mouth open, his neck and chest covered with blood, Nash lay in the front seat. Reed's bloody body slumped in the back seat. Policeman Fannning was the first to arrive after the gangsters fled.

"Get out," he yelled, after opening a car door and pointing a pistol on the lawmen inside.

"Don't shoot, I'm a federal officer," said Smith, putting up his hands.[12]

On his left, Lackey, hit three times in the back, was in great pain.

"Steady now, steady. You'll make it all right," Smith said to Lackey.[13]

Vetterli arrived, helped to take Lackey out of the car, and put him on the ground. Smith held Lackey's head.

"I'll be all right. Look after the others," Lackey insisted.[14]

Dozens of businessmen, taxi drivers, farmers, and others gathered, walking in a swelling pool of blood. Some of them screamed, including a woman wire service reporter wearing blood-stained white shoes. Soon, ambulances came, and rushed Lackey to Research Hospital, where he recovered. Vetterli, still bleeding from his arm wound, ran to the FBI office and called Director J. Edgar Hoover in Washington.[15]

"It was a massacre, Mr. Hoover," Vetterli said, "Ray Caffrey is dead. Joe Lackey may not pull through. Two Kansas City detectives, and the Chief of Police of McAlester, Oklahoma, were killed. So was Frank Nash."[16]

Hoover asked him how he was.

"Well, I lost a good summer coat and a shirt...No, I didn't go to the hospital...Yes, sir, I'll go to a doctor at once."[17]

An agent went to Caffrey's apartment to tell his wife the tragic news. In the Union Station parking lot, FBI agents interviewed witnesses to the massacre. They told several different stories, such as the number of gunmen and descriptions of the killers. Frances Nash, wife of Frank Nash, heard about the massacre on the radio, became upset and fled the area.[18]

"I can't believe it; I can't believe it," Frances said again and again.[19]

Miller awakened his girl friend, Vivian Mathias, who thought he was alone, when he got home about 9 AM. She knew something bad had happened, but she asked no questions. His friend, Fritz Mulloy, came over and drove Vivian and her daughter, Betty, to his house for breakfast. After breakfast, Miller called and asked Vivian to come back home, but to leave Betty at Mulloy's house. Mulloy was told that they were leaving Kansas City and asked him to take care of their possessions for some time. During the cab ride home, the driver told Vivian about the massacre at Union Station.

Upon arriving home Vivian saw two strange men, one of whom Miller called Floyd. (Later, she identified Floyd and Richetti from photos.) Floyd, with a wound in his left shoulder, lay in a bed.

A very upset Miller told her they had been to the station to free Frank Nash, but there had been a gunfight; Frank was killed, and Floyd wounded. Vivian made breakfast, but none of them wanted anything to eat. Miller and Richetti drank coffee. The two gangsters remained in the bedroom all day. She said nothing to them about what had happened, and they, too, said nothing. Sometime during the day Miller, said that his car had gone to and from Union Station. Miller read in the daily newspaper that five or six men had been involved in the shootout.[20]

"That's what the newspapers can do," he said.[21]

Alone, after dark, Miller left the house, looking for Johnny Lazia. Finally, he saw him at the scene of the massacre. Lazia was having dinner with James LaCapra and other friends at the Fred Harvey Restaurant in Union Station.[22] Miller told Lazia Floyd needed medical help, and he and Richetti needed a safe escort out of town.[23] About twenty minutes after Miller returned home, Floyd and Richetti left.[24]

Miller, Vivian, and Betty fled the next day to the gangster Volney Davis's, apartment in Maywood, Illinois. Miller told him he tried to free Nash with the help of "a good man," Charley Floyd. Although he said little about the massacre, he said that he could have successfully gotten Nash had the officers not reached for their guns. That made it a kill or be killed situation, and Miller and his companions then opened fire. Millier did not mention Richetti. The gangster then took a plane to New York City, and Vivian and Betty went to Vivian's parents in Brainerd, Minnesota.[25]

Lazia brought medical aid to Floyd. Then, Lazia's boys asked Floyd if he could travel. They could see he had lost a lot of blood. Floyd grabbed his machine gun, raised it into firing position, and declared, "I can handle this baby."[26]

"Eddie and I are gonna get out of here and lay low for a while," Floyd said.

Richetti added, "Yeah, all we need now is a car."[27]

Late on Monday evening, June 19, Lazia setup an escort to take them out of Kansas City onto Highway 40 and east toward St. Louis. They easily rode in a Buick sedan though the police net around the city.[28]

The Kansas City Massacre was sensational news. Many editorials angrily insisted that gangsters be wiped out. The *Boston Transcript* asked, "In what other civilized country could such a thing happen? Right in the center of a large city, in front of a union station?"[29]

It crystallized many changes for the better. There were new laws, and more money for law enforcement. J. Edgar Hoover would become a major public official, and the FBI would soon become a powerful national police organization.[30]

CHAPTER 4

A PETTY THIEF

George Linus McKeever was born April 26, 1900, in Winchester, Illinois, to Henry P. and Cara B. McKeever. His father, an alcoholic, who was often unemployed, was variously a farmer, a kiln operator in a cement factory, a carpenter, and a gasoline engineer. The couple had four other children: Henry Leo, born in Illinois in 1895; Eloy, born in Illinois, in 1897; Mary T., born in Illinois in 1902; and Milton, born in South Dakota in 1909.[1]

By 1910, the family was living in Sioux City, Iowa, at the navigational head of the Missouri River.[2] The city had an economic boom in the early 20th century, with its population increasing from about 50,000 in 1910 to over 70,000 in 1920. Incorporated in 1858, it was a frontier post on the Missouri River, that was a trade center for farmers and ranchers. Sioux City was one of the major financial, transportation, commercial, industrial and educational centers of the Missouri Valley at that time.[3]

McKeever, raised as a Catholic, went to the excellent Sioux City public schools, but left school after the seventh grade. He then had steady work as a cook for a few years. In the late 1910s, the family moved to Fort Madison, Iowa.[4]

In September 1920, McKeever left home, went to Seattle, Washington, and enlisted in the Marine Corps at the Mare Island, California, Marine Recruit Depot. While in the Marine Corps, he contracted syphilis. McKeever served as a mail guard in California, Portland, Oregon, and Norfolk, Virginia, and was a member of the Marine boxing team.

McKeever had a mixed record and often was in trouble. On March 27, 1921, he was charged with "Disobedience to Cpl. of the Guard," with "insolence and using vile names." At his trial on April 1, he plead guilty, and his Commanding officer gave him thirty days of solitary confinement and a $30 fine. Two months later, on May 21, McKeever stole a book entitled

Captain Billy's Whiz Bang, worth 25 cents. He again plead guilty and received a $30 fine. On September 20, he was charged with "Disobedience of Orders of a Sentry," and was given two weeks restriction by his commanding officer. McKeever was "Under intoxicating liquors" on February 10, 1922.

However, McKeever also received some good reports, such as "character is good." As a Mess Man and prison guard, he was rated excellent. The young man was discharged from duty on August 29, 1922.[5]

After his Marine service, McKeever drifted around by freight train. Often he had no money. A North Dakota judge wrote, "His past record does not show this man to be the type of a man that is a bank robber."[6]

In November 1922, McKeever was told by the police to leave town six hours after he was caught evading railroad fares in San Diego, California. The next month, he was arrested for bootlegging, put in jail for five days, and paid a five dollar fine at an unknown location.[7]

In Los Angeles in January 1923, McKeever was a suspect in a murder. On January 19, in Oakland, California, he was sentenced to 30 days in jail for vagrancy by begging.

In May, McKeever was arrested in Oskaloosa, Iowa, for disturbing the peace at the Rock Island Depot; he spent one day in jail.[8]

The only jobs McKeever was ever known to have were around 1925 in Chicago, when he worked setting up pins in a bowling alley, and as a waiter for eight months at Thompson's Cafeteria. He was arrested twice during that period. Both times he lost his job when Chicago police questioned him. On March 16, 1927, he was arrested in Evanston, Illinois, for investigation, and was jailed for one day.[9]

On Saturday, June 8, 1928, McKeever, James E. Hanley, and Helen Larson were siphoning gasoline from a truck into a can in Mason City, Iowa. A. H. Skellinger, the truck's owner, his wife, and son Howard, saw them when they returned home at 10 P.M.. Skellinger picked up an iron bar, and with his son, Howard, approached the criminals, and asked them what they were doing. Helen Larson was seated in a Studebaker parked nearby.

The criminals offered to pay for the stolen gasoline and asked that they not be turned over to the police, but Skellinger told them he was going to hold them until the police came.

McKeever then attacked him and Skellinger hit McKeever in the head with the iron bar. Meanwhile, Mrs. Skellinger went to their house and called the police.

The three criminals were arrested and taken to the police station. Hanley told police he served in the World War. In their Studebaker, two .38-caliber revolvers, cartridges, clothing, and papers were discovered. A few notebooks tended to corroborate Hanley's statement that he was employed by an electric sign company. Literature claimed by McKeever as his own showed that he was interested in the Industrial Workers of the World, a radical labor union.

When questioned by the acting Chief of Police, the trio told stories that failed to agree as to their past whereabouts. Larson said she had been working in Des Moines, Iowa, and Hanley had gone there to pick her up; while Hanley denied ever having been in that city.

McKeever and Hanley were sentenced by a police court judge to serve ten days in the county jail on the charge of stealing 83 cents of gasoline. McKeever was given an additional sentence of 30 days on the charge of assault and battery. After fingerprints and a mug shot, McKeever spent 40 days in jail.[10]

On May 29, 1929, McKeever was arrested for investigation in St. Paul, and was jailed for four days. The gangster was again arrested there on December 8, 1929, for transporting liquor, but was released the same day.

McKeever's father died in 1929; his mother was living in Burlington, Iowa. About this time, George McKeever started to gamble, especially betting on horse races,[11] and married a woman named Pearl.[12] The next year, on May 15, he was arrested in Mason City, Iowa, for investigation, and then released.[13]

CHAPTER 5

"ONE OF THE CLEVEREST AND MOST EFFICIENT GANGS OF BANK ROBBERS"

I n the early 1930s, McKeever started to rob banks. Very poor, he had been financially desperate for several years. At first, he joined the Reinhold Engel Gang, "one of the cleverest and most efficient gangs of bank robbers," according to the *Huron* SD *Evening Huronite*.[1] The 47-year-old Engel was a debonair leader, who had connections with a Toledo liquor syndicate that paid for his huge $25,000 bail when arrested for some unknown reason. The large gang of about twelve members had robbed dozens of banks in the mid-west since 1925. One member, Phil Ray, claimed he had robbed 37 banks, some with the gang and some alone.[2]

With Engel, Phil Ray, and Sidney Raycraft, McKeever robbed the Citizens National Bank of Wahpeton, North Dakota on May 29, 1930. A bandit remained in a black Hudson sedan parked in the rear of the bank in an alley. The three other men entered the bank after a customer. One of the men placed a gun in the customer's stomach and ordered him to lie down. He then went to teller, Al Bader, and pointed his gun at him.

"Get down quick," he said to Bader and everyone else.

Meeting in a back room was the bank's Board of Directors, who were considering bids for a new bank building. McKeever went to the back room, and ordered the Directors to go to the front of the bank and lie down. Four Directors, six bank employees, and two customers then lay on the floor. As the gang was grabbing $6,735.58 in silver and currency from the money drawers and vault, two other customers came into the bank, but they were able to escape and spread the alarm.[3]

"If anyone sets off an alarm before we get out, we will blow up somebody," yelled a bandit.[4]

Nevertheless, employee Bernard McCusher turned on the alarm. Unable to leave through the locked back door, the bandits then went out the front door. McCusher followed the robbers out of the bank, firing a .32-calier revolver at them. As they entered their car, the gangsters fired a stream of lead behind them, breaking the glass of the car's windows as they shot. A bullet struck the window of Bugbee's Drug Store, and another smashed through the window of Dr. G. Jarobs office, passing between the doctor and a patient he was examining, and smashing a small mirror in the room. Travelling salesman, O. M. Shrane Minneapolis, was struck in the leg and a bullet tore his coat. McCuster jumped into a car with another man, and the two followed the getaway car, but soon lost them.[5]

On August 14, 1930, three men, including McKeever, stole about $7,000 from the Bank of Gretna in Gretna, Nebraska. The Pretty Boy Floyd Gang, however, again was believed to be the culprits. Cool and polite, the unmasked gangsters drew up half a block from the bank in a black Hupmobile sedan with a white and grey license plate. One of them waited in the car.

McKeever and the other man entered the bank, drew guns, and ordered three employees to lie on the floor. McKeever put cash, a .45-caliber gun, and gold into a black bag; the other bandit stood guard at the front door. The three employees and a farmer, who had entered the bank during the robbery, were forced to go into the vault; fortunately, the bank had had air holes drilled only a few weeks before. After fleeing out the back door, the robbers encountered two men at a barber shop. One of them asked, "What do you have in the bag?" They did not reply.

Instead, the bandits fled north in their car, and vanished without a trace.[6]

At noon on January 12, 1931, Engel, McKeever, Henry Kurns, and Max Hetke parked their car at the Grantsburg, Wisconsin, train depot. They planned to commit the only robbery of the First State Bank of Grantsburg. Engel, the driver, stayed behind to protect the car. McKeever, Kurns, and Hetke jumped out, and hurried one block to the bank. The well-dressed robbers wore dark overcoats and silk neck scarves; two had on caps, and one, a hat. Armed with revolvers and a shotgun, they entered the bank. While one bandit covered four bank employees, and five customers, the other two grabbed silver, gold, and currency worth $12,000 from the cash drawers.

The prisoners were forced into the vault, but this time the bandits could not lock it, and then fled. An alarm was immediately spread throughout the region. Posses were quickly organized to search north of Grantsburg, where the bandits were believed to have gone.

Bank employees thought, "The calm and precise manner in which they conducted the holdup were indications that the men... were no novices at the game...."[7]

Two days later, in front of Engel's St. Paul home, Engel Gang member, Edward Carnes, killed Chicago gangster Thomas "Crooked Nose" Melnick over a dispute about loot. Engel, Carnes, and other gang members were arrested and questioned by police, but soon released. Carnes was later convicted of slaying Melnick.[8]

At 9 A.M. on March 10, 1931, McKeever robbed the Farmers Savings Bank of Alden, Iowa, of $4,000 in cash and negotiable securities, with Engel and Kurns. Two shabbily dressed unmasked men, with their hats pulled down their foreheads, entered the bank. One was about 40 years old and five feet ten inches tall, while the other was about 30 years old and slightly taller. Both were too tall to be McKeever, who waited outside in a car. Inside the bank were dentist R. C. Roberts, cashier, W. H. Miller, assistant cashier, LeLand H. Waton, and bank teller Otto Copping.

The employees and dentist were ordered to lie on the floor and told they would be shot if they moved. After Miller gave them the money, and the men were forced into the vault, the criminals fled. The robbery took twelve minutes. Using an inside release, the prisoners soon fled the vault, and spread the alarm.[9]

A few days later, Engel, and Hetke were arrested for the Grantsburg robbery. Hetke confessed he, Engel, Kurns, and McKeever committed that crime. Police in the midwest searched for Kurns and McKeever. On March 24, 1931, the Burnett County, Wisconsin, Circuit Court sentenced Engel to fifteen to forty years at the Wisconsin State Prison, while Hetke received a fifteen to twenty year sentence.[10] Engel appealed his sentence, and was freed under $25,000 bail on April 27, 1931, paid for by the Toledo liquor syndicate.[11]

Engel Gang members Engel, Ray, Raycraft, and Van Tress stole $1,550 in cash and $17,000 in registered bonds from the Bank of Ipswich in Ipswich, South Dakota, on the morning of May 18, 1932. The bandits pulled their guns when they entered the bank.

"Stick 'em up!" they yelled.

Bank President, M. Beebe, jumped on one of the men, grabbed him around the neck, and started a fight. The bandit hit Beebe over his head with a gun, and then fired at him. Beebe was wounded in both thighs, and fell to the floor. He was taken to the hospital, where he eventually made a total recovery.

"He was a fool to resist," one of the bandits later said.

Cashier, Chester Doolittle, taken as a hostage, was released at 7 P.M. that night near Buford, South Dakota.[12]

Two days later, in South Paul, Minnesota, Van Tress hit a lamppost with the getaway car, eluding a police car. He was captured after hiding in a rooming house attic. Van Tress gave a complete confession, and told where the robbers were staying in St. Paul. George McKeever was fingered, but not found. The police recovered all money, and each of the robbers were arrested and confessed. All received thirty years in the South Dakota State Penitentiary.[13]

CHAPTER 6

"I DID NOT ROB ANY BANKS"

During the winter of 1932 George McKeever formed a new gang consisting of himself, Francis McNeiley, his brother Eloy, and Lee Bostetter; their headquarters was on a Cherrydale, Missouri, farm.[1]

Francis McNeiley, born in Wayne County, Iowa, on July 16, 1911, to farmer Saeltzer Burgh and Flora Ethel McNeiley, was a Iowa farm laborer looking for work. According to many, he did not look like a killer.[2] His parents had four other children: Finus, Burgh, Jr., Clara and Anne.[3]

Wayne County bordered Missouri to the south. Given legal status in 1874, its peak population was 1600 in 1913, with few minorities. Like most farm families in the county, the McNeileys were poor. A network of paved "farmer to market" roads went out from Allerton, the county seat, to connect nearby towns. The town, plotted in 1870, was a division point on the Chicago, Rock Island, & Pacific Railroad.[4]

Helen B. Lewis, McNeiley's seventh grade teacher, said that "I can truthfully say that I never worked with a finer boy." Missouri State Senator, Nick Cave, and Howard P. Major, his defense attorneys, each said McNeiley was not the criminal type. Neighbors, teachers, and friends supported the young man. Oscar P. Puckett, Superintendent of the Allerton School System, characterized McNeiley as, "a clean, modest boy, who never gave us any trouble."[5]

In the late 1920s, the McNeiley family moved to Des Moines, Iowa, where the father was an apartment custodian, and Francis attended high school.[6]

Eloy McKeever, never imprisoned or convicted of a crime, married McNeiley's 15-year-old Sister, in 1931. Francis became angry at Eloy for mistreating his sister. Formerly an auto mechanic in Des Moines from 1922 to 1932, One day he had a car accident with a Cherryville neighbor, and was arrested. Eloy was now looking for work.[7]

Lee Bostetter was easy to identify because he only had one eye. In 1910, he was born into the farm family of Elmer and Minnie Bostetter, in Michell, Iowa. Almost all of his family were criminals and became known as "The Bostetter Gang."[8]

The so-called "McKeever Gang" held up the Bank of Lucerne at Lucerne, Missouri, at 4 P.M. on January 31, 1933, for $1,588. The Pretty Boy Floyd Gang got the credit for the robbery again. McKeever's gang went to Lucerne in a Ford V-8 coupe with an Iowa tag. George and McNeiley went into the bank, while Eloy stayed in the car. Some people who saw the men in Lucerne during the day, and some who saw them enter the bank, all believed they were bank robbers. Assistant cashier, Valda Stout, the only person in the bank, was forced to lie on the floor. Later, a customer, Mrs. James Soomers, went in and also was told to lie down. While McNeiley took the cash and silver out of the cages, McKeever grabbed the money from the vault. After getting the money, the bandits forced the women into the vault, locked them in, and fled; bank officials later had to open it to free them. Mrs. Stout's father chased the bandits in his car, but soon lost them. Sheriff A. B. Gibson and two deputies went after the bandits, directing officers to guard every road south of Lucerne, but the bandits had fled north. Eight days later, the bank closed. Later, it was said the robbers were arrested for killing policemen.[9]

After the bank robbery, the gang hid in northern Iowa. George McKeever used the alias, Henry Bennett, Eloy McKeever was called Eddie Bennett, and McNeiley's alias was Francis Meyer.[10] Late that spring, McKeever and McNeiley hid together on a farm near Harviell, Missouri. McKeever used the alias, Claud Adams, while McNeiley went by the name Dan Weber. The farm's owner disliked the rude McKeever.

Around June 11, the gangsters left the farm, with McNeiley using the alias, Joe Clark.

McNeiley bought a used, black ford V-8 for $20 in St. Louis. They headed for Columbia, Missouri, on June 13. Short on cash, the bandits planned to rob a store. That night, north of Columbia, they slept in their car. The next morning, the two men drove through the countryside and were seen stopping to repair a tire. Around 3:15 P.M., at a roadblock just north of Columbia, they killed two lawmen.[11]

Eluding the manhunt, McKeever and McNeiley hid for a few weeks at McKeever's mother's home in Burlington, Iowa.[12] In September 1933, McNeiley joined a riverboat crew, going up and down the Mississippi River for several months.[13]

On October 27, 1933, the Bostetter Gang was arrested in Iowa. Lee Bostetter was jailed for a short time. Only his brother Clifford was convicted of a crime, receiving a two to three year sentence for burglary.[14]

McNeiley rejoined the McKeever gang in Burlington, Iowa, in the spring of 1934. George McKeever bragged that he, his brother, Eloy, and Bostetter had dropped out of sight, but had continued to do many "little jobs"; burglaries and stealing cars in Missouri and Iowa. The only news had been the arrest of Bostetter.[15]

On the night of July 23, 1934, the day after John Dillinger was killed, McKeever and McNeiley were Looking for a house to rob in Sioux City, Iowa. Two local detectives saw the two suspicious men, jumped out of their car, and chased them. After one officer fired a few warning shots, McKeever was captured when he slipped and fell. McNeiley escaped.

Charged with "house prowling,' the captured thug gave his name as Paul Adams and his residence as Omaha. Fingerprint evidence showed he was actually George McKeever, who had been "positively identified through fingerprints" of robbing the Farmers Savings Bank of Alden, Iowa, with three other bandits on March 10, 1931.

McKeever told the officers, "You are crazy. I never heard of that place before. I did not rob any banks in North or South Dakota. I never robbed any banks."

On August 9, 1934, a formal request for the extradition of McKeever for the Wahpeton, North Dakota, bank robbery came from North Dakota Governor Clyde L. Herring.[16]

CHAPTER 7

"NOT ONE OF THE WEAPONS"

Major Lewis M. Means of the Missouri Highway Patrol began an intensive search for the killers of lawmen Booth and Wilson. Clues consisted only of the bullets taken from the bodies of the murdered lawmen; a description by four witnesses of the gangsters at the crime scene and the license number of the getaway car.[1] The murderers were identified as Pretty Boy Floyd and Adam Richetti.[2] Merle Gill, a private ballistic expect, in Kansas City, Missouri, was given the bullets from the crime. He discovered they had come from a .38-caliber revolver and a .45-caliber pistol.[3]

Gill was born to Flora H. Gill on July 30, 1897. His father had died before the turn of the century. After graduating from the 8th grade he served in the Navy during World War I. Gill opened his ballistics business in Kansas City, Missouri, in 1927.[4]

Criminals caught in any place in the mid-west with .38-caliber or .45-caliber guns were considered suspects in the murders. Gill carefully examined their weapons; however he always returned them with the same response; "Not one of the weapons."[5]

In a rogues gallery, Major Means of the Missouri National Guard found a "dead ringer" picture for Pretty Boy Floyd, a man named George McKeever, but he did not take the find seriously.[6]

The license plate number of the getaway car at the crossroads murders of lawmen Booth and Wilson was traced to a car dealer in St. Louis who told Means a man named "Joe Clark" brought the car, and was staying in a boarding house in the city. He provided a good description. Means went to the landlady, who could give little information, but did provide a description of the man, which was similar to that given by the car dealer. Means followed every lead, but found nothing.[7]

According to Gill:
For the next several weeks I was buried in my laboratory from early morning until late at night, seven days a week. The FBI, anxious to get a pistol identification, kept pouring in guns on me. One batch alone consisted of 75 weapons which had been seized when several members of the infamous Barrow gang had been rounded up at Platte, Missouri. Other weapons were pistols used by Wilbur Underhill, Harvey Bailey, "Machine Gun" Kelly and many other equally notorious outlaw.

Throughout this period I had many conferences with Major Means and other Investigators working on the Columbia mystery. They were certain that 'Pretty Boy' Floyd and his henchmen had killed the two police officers as a prelude to their participation in the massacre. The whole picture fitted together perfectly. I was confidentially informed, and, furthermore, no less than seven eyewitnesses had picked out photographs of Floyd and Richetti as the two thugs who had so ruthlessly shot down Sheriff Wilson and Sergeant Booth. The identifications were positive and the witnesses were prepared to go into court should either one or both of the outlaws be captured.... ‾

I discovered that one of the /Kansas City Massacre/ pistols had been an army type of .45-caliber Colt's automatic, and the other from a .38-caliber Colt's revolver...Booth had been wounded by the .45, and both he and Wilson killed by the .38. Were the two pistols used in the massacre; the same weapons used in the cross-roads murders?[8]

Gill believed the bullets did not come from the same weapons.[9]

CHAPTER 8

"WITH THEIR GUNS SPITTING BULLETS"

Rumors spread during the summer and fall of 1934 that Pretty Boy Floyd was hiding out on farms in northern Iowa. About this time, three men went there, staying at the Al Bostetter farm, one and a half miles from McIntire, Iowa, a village of 268 people, some six miles from the Minnesota border. The nearest town of any size was Cresco, Iowa. These three men did not work, had "plenty of money," and kept busy hunting pheasants.[1]

One of the men was Lee Bostetter, the farm owner's son. The other two were known as "Ed Bennett" (actually Eloy McKeever) and "Francis Gould" (actually Francis McNeiley). Bennett was related to the Bostetters, known criminals. But Bennett was a quiet man, being very cautious as to what he said and did. Anyone visiting the Bostetter farm was never permitted to look at him closely. There were rumors Gould was Baby Face Nelson, however, he did look like the Dillinger bandit.[2]

About 10 PM on Saturday, August 25, 1934, the unmasked McNeiley, McKeever, and Bostetter, robbed the Godfrey General

Store at Chapin, Iowa. Going in with their guns drawn, the bandits ordered store owner, J. Godfrey, Mrs. Godfrey, their two sons, Clinton and Donald, and several customers, to lie face downward on the floor. McKeever struck Clinton twice on the head with a gun butt when he was slow to lie on the floor. While two of the bandits searched everyone, the third man stood guard. They took $100 from the cash register, as well as about $30 from the two Godfrey boys, and $30 more from a salesman. As the bandits left the store through a side entrance they grabbed flour and sugar sacks.

"Don't be in a hurry to get up," one of them said.

They vanished before an alarm could sound.[3]

On September 28, near Bonair, Iowa, Howard County, Iowa, Deputy Sheriff Will Owens served a notice at the home of Mrs. Fred Webber, a daughter, and saw a man with a heavy growth of whiskers in the yard acting suspiciously, and care-ful to keep some distance from the officer. At first, Deputy Owens did not think anything of it, but he later thought the man was Pretty Boy Floyd. He remembered the man resembled "Public Enemy No. 1" in size, features, and height. No one told the FBI about this man.[4]

Sheriff Tollof, Deputy Owens, and County Attorney Anderson, were all on the case for the next few days. Their purpose was to find the man and his associates, determine their habits, and identify them before arresting them.

The officers discovered the man thought to be Floyd used the name of Ed Bennett, and was with two other men. On several occasions, the three men drove a black V-8 Ford with stolen plates into the Webber yard during the early morning hours. The mysterious Ford always disappeared in the daytime and never stayed in the same yard two nights in succession. The auto was always kept near where the men slept. On October 2, the officials lost track of the men and the car. Three days later Owens called the state police, and State Agent, A G. Height, was sent to help him.[5]

At 3 PM on October 11, Owens and Height, went to the Bostetter farm for a preliminary check-up before actually arresting "Floyd." Owens was driving and saw the car they sought. Going into the yard, they noticed McKeever—believed to be Pretty Boy Floyd—sitting in the car's driver seat, parked next to a cornfield. The gangster realized who they were.

The deputy got out of his car and entered the cornfield to get a better look, while Height stayed in the vehicle. Suddenly, McNeiley and Bostetter leapt into the Ford and quickly sped away. They had a .330 rifle, one of the newest and highest powered rifles then made, and an automatic machine gun. State Agent Height had a rifle with high-speed mushroom bullets (that would explode in the body), and deputy Owens had a .38 revolver, his service weapon.

Owens returned to his car and chased the criminals. On a gravel road, McKeever headed east at high speed. They riddled the gangsters' car with bullets, but rough roads caused the gunfire to go wild. After a sharp but ineffective exchange, McKeever turned down a road that ended at a vacant house.[6] As the bandits fled into the house, they fired at the lawmen. Owens stopped about one hundred feet from the house. The two officers left their car and took cover in nearby woods. The branches blinded them during an exchange of gunfire to their quarry.

After a few minutes, the bandits ran back to their vehicle, went "lickite-split and with their guns spitting bullets," and passed the lawmen. A .45-caliber machine gun bullet came close to killing Owens when it pierced the frame of the officer's car, just four inches above his head. The lawmen fired eighteen shots at the gangsters, and they thought one of them was hit. Turning north when they got to the main road, McKeever "whizzed northward into Minnesota, dodged west," and returned to Iowa.[7]

About seventy shots were fired during the gun duel, the bandits shooting three bullets to the officers' one. The officers shots landed nine times, while only one bullet fired by the gunmen hit the police car. They hit the Ford's engine, the right door, and the back of the auto, which showed several bullet holes. One passed directly parallel to anyone in the back seat. It was not known, however, if anyone was wounded or killed. The lawmen lost them near Richville, Iowa.[8]

Patrols were stationed at strategic points along highways in northern Iowa and southern Minnesota, but the bandits' car stayed missing until about 10 PM, October 12, 1934, when there were reports it had sped through a Missouri border town. FBI agents and Iowa officers joined the hunt late that evening, and set up roadblocks. Near Princeton, Missouri, the gangsters were seen heading for the Ozark hills. Deputy Sheriff Owens told reporters there was "no question" it was Pretty Boy Floyd, who might be wounded or killed, that Baby Face Nelson was not one of Floyd's companions, and that the gangsters almost killed him.[9]

CHAPTER 9

WHO WAS EDDIE BENNETT?

Following the news of the October 1934 gun fight, Missouri Highway Patrol Major Means learned two men (later determined to be Eloy McKeever and McNeily) stopped at a house in Moberly, Missouri, and asked to wash their hands the day after the battle. The lady of the house gave them soap, a towel, and water. While they were cleaning up, one of them inadvertently dropped .38 and .45 cartridges, which were the same kind of bullets at the crossroad murders. They left in a car without the cartridges, which were later given to Major Means.

Means believed these men might have been involved with the Iowa gun battle the day before, as well as the crossroads murders. Means caught an airplane to Cresco, Iowa, to talk to Deputy Owens. The deputy told him he and another lawmen battled with three gangsters, but had lost them going around small country roads.

"I've learned some important information from an acquaintance," Owens said. "We'll talk to him."

The informer said, "I don't know anything about the gun fight. All I know is that I happened to run into some men who fit the description of the men in the gun fight. I had seen them around the county before. I think it was in the spring of 1933. One of them was named Eddie Bennett, and another was Henry Bennett. Another, a short man, was Francis Meyer. Later, Lee Bostetter joined up with them."

"Can you give me a good description of them?" the deputy asked. "Well, Eddie Bennett was the biggest. He had dark hair and his eyes were mean looking. Henry Bennett was short. Bostetter had one eye gone. He used to live around here. Meyer talked more than the rest. He had a father who worked as a janitor in Des Moines: also had a brother who worked in a drugstore there. Meyer told me about working on a steamboat in St. Louis one time. He wore glasses."

"What kind of guns did they have?"

I don't know how many guns they had, but one of them carried a .45 automatic and another a .38. I saw a sawed-off shot gun in their car once, with a high-powered rifle."

"That was the rifle used on us the other day," Owens remarked, "One of them riddled our car as we ran them into a side road."

Means became excited when he heard this. The description of Meyer was very close to that of Joe Clark, an alias of McNeiley. He knew Sheriff Wilson had been killed by a .38 long bullet fired from a .38 police special. Patrolman Booth was shot through the heart by such a bullet; Wilson, the head. A .45-caliber automatic bullet had been in Booth's leg. Means admitted this was weak evidence. When Means used the names he had of the gangsters in a search of local and state records, he found nothing.[1]

Mr. and Mrs. Bostetter, their daughter Alice, and two others, were taken to Cresco on October 13, and grilled by federal men and county officials for a day and night. The Bostetter family had moved to McIntire about two years earlier. They had known the man claimed to be Pretty Boy Floyd for several years as a distant relative named Ed Bennett, but the family had no knowledge of his occupation or his home. Their son Lee had been with them for two years. The prisoners were temporarily released.[2]

About this time, Pretty Boy Floyd was killed, Richetti captured in Ohio. Deputy Owens later talked with Richetti at the Columbia, Missouri, jail and was more firmly convinced than ever he and Floyd had nothing to do with the Booth-Wilson killings.

Colonel Casteel, Commander of the Missouri Highway Patrol, let Means return to Iowa, after he told the Commander he was hot on the trail of the two murderers. He investigated every lead and questioned many people, often with Deputy Owens. The lawmen learned that on October 12, the day after the pursuit, three men bought a new Ford V-8 in Leon, Iowa. When they were asked about the hundred dollar bills the men had used to pay, they fled in the new vehicle. Their descriptions fit what Means was looking for. Officers believed the car purchaser may have been Pretty Boy Floyd.

Police found an old completely burned, mud-spattered, bullet-ridden Ford V-8 with an Iowa license plate on the night of October 13 near Numa, Iowa, some fifty miles from Leon. Agent Height drove to Numa, and identified the car as being the same one used by "Floyd" in the gun battle. The tires were removed, so they would burn completely, the radio and a shortwave set had been removed, the speed meter reader was destroyed; and the car had been completely burned with kerosene. Several raincoats, a suit of brown clothes, three leather suitcases, and two tan suitcases were near the vehicle.[3]

Two men, answering to the description of two of the three men involved in the gun battle, robbed a bank in Hawarden, Iowa, on the afternoon of October 16. The car used in the robbery was identical to the one purchased in Leon, Iowa, by the bandit believed to be Pretty Boy Floyd. Iowa State agent Height went directly to Hawarden to aid in the bank robbery investigation.[4]

Again Means heard about Henry Bennett, and learned he, his brother, Eddie, and Lee Bostetter lived on a farm in Cherryville, Missouri, during 1932. State troopers sent to Cherryville to investigate discovered that after Eddie Bennett had been in a car accident with a neighbor, he had been arrested. Fortunately, the arrest record had the car's license number. Motor vehicle records showed that the car had been sold to a Fort Madison, Iowa, man. When questioned by Means, the man at first provided little information, but finally revealed the real name of "Eddie Bennett": Eloy McKeever. Means also knew McKeever had relatives in Burlington, Iowa, and that "Eddie Bennett" had married the sister of "Francis Meyer." Checking marriage records he found McKeever had married Anne McNeiley, the sister of Francis McNeiley. Soon, he knew the real name of "Henry Bennett": George McKeever.[5]

CHAPTER 10

"ONE OF THE MOST FIENDISH CRIMES"

O n the very cold, dark night of Saturday, October 20, 1934, Eloy McKeever, Bostetter and McNeiley robbed a general store in Johnsburg, Minnesota. Two weeks previous, McKeever had purchased beer at the same store. Johnsburg, consisting of a general store, a large Catholic Church and a few houses, was near the Iowa state line. With McKeever driving, the three men reached the general store at 9:10 PM. McKeever and McNeiley, wearing dark hats and dark suits, entered the store. Bostetter, wearing a light gray suit, stayed in the getaway car.

Sixty-year-old storekeeper, John Freund, swept the floor near some flour sacks in front of the store, while his friend, John Kresback, listened to the radio in the back room. McKeever and McNeiley entered the store, pulled their guns, and ordered Freund to hold up his hands. He did so. McNeily told Kresback to hand over his money.

"I am broke," replied Kresback.[1]

The bandits searched him, but found nothing; they missed $14 on him. Kresback was forced to lie on the floor.

"Turn and open the safe," McKeever yelled to Freund.

"My son, Isadore, who is next door, has the safe's combination. I have to go over and get him," replied the storekeeper.[2]

When Freund started to go through a side door to his living quarters, calling for Isadore, McKeever grabbed him, and they struggled. McNeiley came up and hit Freund several times on the head with the butt of his revolver.

"Aw—Plug 'em," screamed McNeiley.

While McNeiley held him, his partner put his huge German Luger pistol to the back of Freund's neck and fired. The bullet passed downwards through Freund's neck, coming out on the left side of the body just above the heart. He died instantly. Blood spattered on the criminals.[3] Later it was determined even if McKeever had not shot Freund he would have died from a crushed skull.[4]

Isadore heard the shot, and tried to open the door from the other side.

"You better stay there," ordered one of the bandits.

Bostetter came into the store and grabbed two cartons of cigarettes and $20. The trio ran out of the store and fled.[5] A man in a parked car saw the getaway vehicle sped away.

Kresback got up, notified some village residents, and, then, called the local telephone operator.[6]

Shortly after 9:30 PM, Becker County, Minnesota, Sheriff Charles Katban got the call from the Stacyville, Iowa, telephone operator to go to Johnsburg to investigate the crime. The Sheriff went with a Deputy and was joined in Stacyville by local Marshal, Ray Giles. In questioning Kresback and Freund's son Isadore, they learned two men entered the store, robbed the till, and struck and killed the store owner. Fingerprints were taken.

The officers traced the getaway car by following its tire tracks on dirt roads to Stacyville, and north to Rose Creek, Minnesota. There, the trail was lost among similar tread marks on the road. The license number and make of car was unknown. Some thought that the Pretty Boy Floyd gang was responsible.[7]

Johnsburg citizens reported Freund always said that, if any person attempted to rob him, he would put his hands up and tell them to take anything they wanted.

"Freund was cruelly murdered and without any good reason," remarked his friend, Kresback. A local newspaper wrote it was, "one of the most fiendish crimes in this section for many years."[8]

Officers in southern Minnesota and northern Iowa were still on the lookout for the murderers on Monday, October 22. Sheriff Syck of Austin, Minnesota, said he was working on some important angles of the case, but was not prepared to make an announcement. An "early break" was expected."[9]

An autopsy was performed at the E. P. Hattens Funeral Home in Stacyville. According to the autopsy report Freund would have died from a crushed skull caused by McNeiley, even if Eloy McKeever had not shot him.[10] Funeral services for Freund were held on October 23 at St. Johns Church, and burial that day was at the church's cemetery. An inquest was held nine days later. Freund was survived by his son Isadore and two daughters.[11] On October 27, the Mower County, Minnesota, government offered a $ 400 reward for the arrest of the storekeeper's slayers. Freund, a widower, was born on July 29, 1875, near Meyer, Iowa. His father had started the Johnsburg General Store. In 1918, John Freund had become the store's owner when his father died.[12]

McNeiley later said, "After we got away from them after the car chase, we hung around Iowa until the first of November when I went to work for the farmer where Major Means arrested me. Eloy and Lee came there and were going to make me go with them, but I told them I was through and was going to stay there. If the law came, it would just have to come.

They left and that's the last I saw of them."

According to the farm owner, "Eloy and Lee had a row with Francis. He pulled a gun on them because he didn't want to go with them. He said he was done."[13]

CHAPTER 11

"I BELIEVE THIS IS NOT THE TIME TO COMPROMISE WITH CRIMINALS"

On November 13, 1934, North Dakota State Attorney, Clifford Schneller, and a lawman, went to Sioux City, Iowa, to take George McKeever to the Wahpeton, North Dakota, jail. The next day, McKeever's trial began with a jury selection. Schneller handled the case. Judge M. McKenna appointed the Johnson & Miller Law Firm to defend McKeever. McKeever pled not guilty to bank robbery.[1]

The State's first witnesses took the stand the following morning. Bank cashier, S. H. Murray, described the Wahpeton bank hold-up, and identified McKeever as one of this bank robbers. Minneapolis contractor A. J. Moorman, in the Directors' room during the robbery, identified McKeever as the bandit who entered the Directors' room, marched the Directors out, and made them lie on the lobby floor. Bank director, J. P. Powrie, also identified the gangster as one of the bandits.

Defense Counsel sought discrepancies in the testimony order to weaken identification of McKeever as one of the bandits. They also cross-examined the witnesses.[2]

The next day, three more witnesses testified for the state. Wahpeton businessman, Henry P. Holthusen, identified McKeever, saying he was at his business door when the bandits ran to the get-away car, firing their weapons only a few feet away. He believed McKeever was one of them. Bank Director, George Reeder, also was sure McKeever was there.

Burns Detective Agency Officer, W. S. Gordon, instrumental in apprehending McKeever, went next to the stand. He told about two confessed robbers of the Wahpeton bank, Phil Ray and Sidney Roycraft, who fingered McKeever as another one of the robbers, and about McKeever's arrest in Sioux City, Iowa.

The State ended its case, and the Defense Counsel immediately began testimony. Tellers Earl Robinson and Al Bader could not identify McKeever, saying they did not have the opportunity to see all of the robbers. Prominent Wahpeton wholesale merchant, George Reeder, testified that McKeever looked like the bandit and was the same weight and height; but, after four years, he could not positively say he was the same bandit. Cashier Murray also said he could not answer that question after all these years. The jury went out and soon came back with a guilty verdict.[3]

On November 20, the handcuffed McKeever, quiet and calm, was taken by two deputies into the courthouse and seated in one of the jury chairs next to his counsel, Vernon M. Johnson.

State Attorney Schneller appeared before the court and said he had no sympathy for McKeever because he had wounded an innocent victim in the robbery. In another robbery of the bank two young women were taken as hostages and badly injured.[4]

"I do not believe this is the time to compromise with criminals or the type of criminal before the court," Schneller asserted. He concluded by asking the court to sentence McKeeveer to the fullest extent of the law.[5]

Defense counsel Johnson said:

> I believe the jurors acted to the best of their ability, but it
> must be realized that the defendant was unable to bring
> in any witnesses from outside the state. I was appointed to
> defend McKeever on one afternoon and went to trial with
> the case the following afternoon. A number of people had
> the opportunity to identify the men perhaps more closely
> than the witnesses called but they could not appear before
> the court to testify that McKeever was not one of the rob-
> bers. One witness asserted he was not the man but would
> not place her testimony against that of the group who did
> indentify McKeever.[6] Johnson asserted that the witnesses
> who identified McKeever four and a half years after the rob-
> bery could not describe other events accurately, and he did
> not believe McKeever to have had sufficient witnesses.

"This was the poorest type of evidence in a c riminal action,"
Johnson continued. "This man comes into this court an indigent,
alone without friends, against a case built up solely on identity. He
is not the type of criminal who robs banks in spite of the fact he
has been compared to Dillinger and Floyd and others."

Johnson then pled for a short sentence for McKeever on the
basis he would return to society a better individual. He concluded
by saying McKeever's life was not such as to warrant taking him
from society for any great length of time.[7]

Judge McKeena questioned McKeever, who said he had been
away from home since he was 16-years-old. He admitted a number
of aliases, such as George Baker, Paul Adams and George Burns.
McKeever then told them the major events of his life.

The judge read a letter from the Iowa Buireau of Criminal
Investigation that identified McKeever as one of the robbers of a
bank in Alden, Iowa. McKeever denied this, and asserted he had

been falsely identified, and had been falsely accused of other bank robberies. A letter from the U. S. Department of Justice, enumerating a long list of arrests for petty larcenies, vagrancy, and investigations, was also read.

"You practically haven't done an honest day's work since 1922," the judge told the prisoner. McKeever described a few jobs where he had been employed, but admitted he had not worked a great deal. He denied any acquaintance with Dillinger. Only for the past five years, he said, had he been a gambler.

"Your personal appearance, habits, or company must have been strange to have been in jail so often," the court then asserted.

"I never thought I h ad exceptional features," McKeever answered. "I have been mistaken for other men before, but never with such disastrous results as this."

The court questioned him about his not knowing where he was on May 29, 1930, the day of the Wahpeton robbery, to which the defendant answered there were a great number of days in the past when he could not now remember where he was.

Not favoring long prison sentences, the judge sentenced McKeever to ten years in the state penitentiary. He believed the gangster would realize that the court was sentencing him as though he had never been in trouble before.[8]

George McKeever

Author's Collection

GEORGE McKEEVER
Defendant in Murder Trial

Author's Collection

George McKeever

Personal Collection

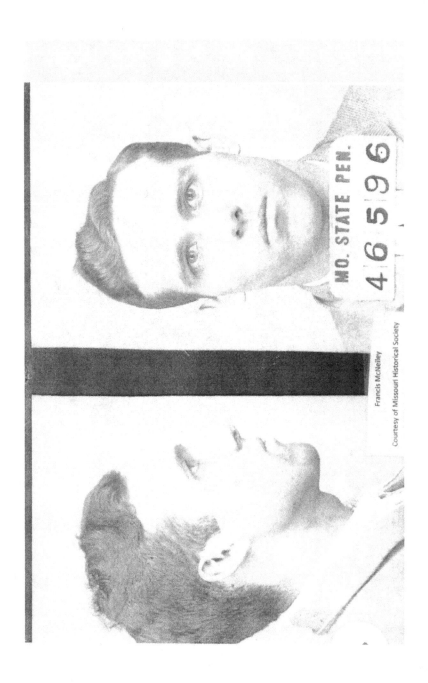

Francis McNeiley

Courtesy of Missouri Historical Society

Francis McNeiley

Author's Collection

Boone County, Missouri, Sheriff Roger Wilson

Courtesy of Law enforcement Officer's Memorial

Missouri Highway Patrol Sergeant Benjamin Booth

Courtesy of Law enforcement Officer's Memorial

Charles "Pretty Boy" Floyd

Courtesy of FBI

Adam Richetti

Courtesy of FBI

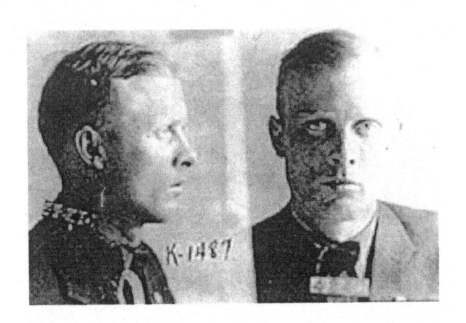

Verne Miller

Courtesy of the FBI

A crossroads at Columbia, Missouri, where George McKeever and Francis
McNeiley murdered Sheriff Roger Wilson of Boone County, Missouri, and
Missouri Highway Patrol Sergeant Benjamin Booth

Author's Collection

I have lived in this community a great many years, but I have never known any tragedy that has so affected the entire community as this one has."

GEORGE S. STARRETT
Columbia attorney in 1933

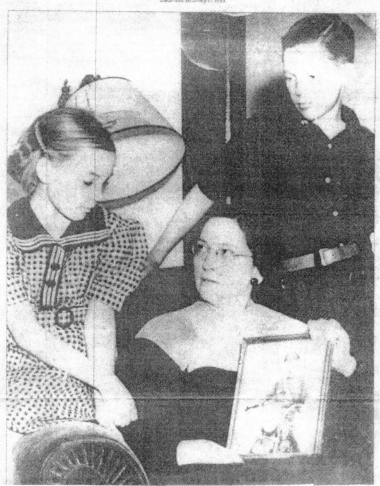

Sally Booth, Widow of Benjamin Booth, and their children

Massillon, Ohio, The evening Independent, Sept. 26th, 1935

Kansas City Massacre/"Pretty Boy" Floyd

Scene in front of the Kansas City railroad depot moments after the attack.

Courtesy of FBI

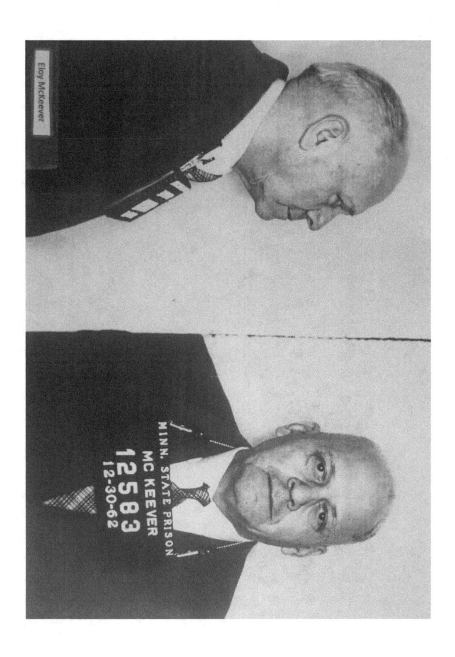

ANNE McKEEVER

Sister of Francis Mcneiley, Wife of Eloy Mckeever

Author's Collection

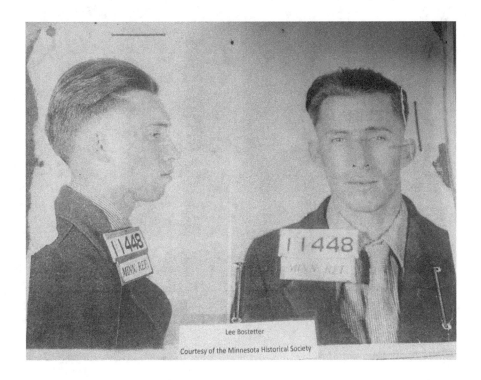

Lee Bostetter
Courtesy of the Minnesota Historical Society

Merle Gill, Noted Ballistican

Author's Collection

Missouri Highway Patrol Captain Lewis Means (Left) used an

airplane in the manhunt for McKeever and McNeiley

Author's Collection

PART TWO

CHAPTER 12

THE BIG BREAK

I n November 1934, Missouri Highway Patrol Major Lewis Means, took a trip to Burlington, Iowa, and located McKeever's relatives. He learned from reliable sources that Eloy McKeever and a friend frequently came to Burlington and stayed around for days at a time.

They usually drove good cars, and dressed well.

Means then checked all of the McNeileys in Des Moines, and found one man who had a son by the name of Francis. He discovered Francis at times came to his father's apartment with two other men and stayed there. One of the men fit Eloy McKeever's description, and the other looked like his younger brother, George McKeever. An informer believed McNeiley was working on a farm near Allerton, Iowa.[1]

The lawman went to Allerton, and contacted another informer, who knew McNeiley and where he was staying. Since it was raining heavy and the unpaved roads were impassable, Means returned to Missouri. Means called Park Findly, the Superintendent of the Iowa Bureau of Investigation, who assigned him two officers.

On November 25, 1934, Means, wearing a disguise of old clothes, met Wayne County, Iowa, Sheriff J. E. McDonald, and the

Wayne County Attorney at Corydon, the county seat. They agreed Means and the sheriff would arrest McNeiley that night at the farm where he worked.[2]

In heavy rain, the lawmen drove to the farm, where the car slipped, spun around, and stopped. After leaping out and entering the farmhouse, they found only a young man standing just inside; they patted him down. A .45 Colt automatic was found on him, and nearby was an automatic shotgun.

"We've some questions we'd like to ask you, Francis," Means told him. "Do you mind?"

"Not at all."[3]

They went to his room, where they found a .30 Luger, a .38 pistol, and plenty of ammunition. The .38 pistol was not his, McNeiley insisted. Looking around the house, the officers found scattered car parts, maps of several towns, lots of ammunition, auto paint, radiator caps, and tire covers. They thought these were stolen car parts.

Afterwards, the lawmen drove to Corydon. They began to question McNeiley about his work, his life, and any crimes he may have committed. With them, were the two Iowa officers. They learned little, except that his farm boss was in Corydon; he was picked up and questioned. He told them the always armed Bostetter, Eloy, and McNeiley often came to his farm. McNeiley was questioned again.[4]

"We knew you are not a Sunday School boy, and you should come clean, as we would find out what he had done," Means told him.[5]

The gangster admitted he had helped rob a Lucerne, Missouri, bank, and a store near Waterloo, Iowa; and that he was with Eloy McKeever, and Bostetter at the October 11 gun battle, and during the murder of a Johnsburg, Minnesota, storekeeper.

Means called Sheriff Ira W. Syuk of Austin, Minnesota, telling him they had a man who confessed he was one of the three men at the Johnsburg murder.

"I will send down an eyewitness, John Kresback," the sheriff said.

After the eyewitness identified McNeiley as one of the men at the murder scene, Means asked the gangster if he had killed Booth and Wilson. McNeiley admitted he had done so and that Eloy McKeever had been with him; but, later, the lawmen found that Eloy had been working at Keokuk, Iowa, the day of the murders.

After being returned to the Columbia jail, McNeiley made a second confession on December 18, indicating his partner in the murders was George McKeever. The reason he had at first said Eloy was with him, was because he wanted revenge, since Eloy had mistreated his sister, and should have given him more money from their robberies. McNeiley then went into great detail about the events of June 14, 1933.

Means took the .45-caliber gun confiscated from McNeiley and sent a bullet from that gun to Kansas City, Missouri, ballistician Merle Gill, who compared the bullet with a bullet taken from one of Sergeant Booth's legs. Gill found both bullets came from the same gun.[6]

CHAPTER 13

"I SEE YOU HAVE QUITE A STORE HERE"

On Saturday, December 22, 1934, Eloy McKeever and Lee Bostetter robbed the Skogland Drug Company at Ida Grove, Iowa, just as the store was about to close a few minutes before midnight. Mrs. Bostetter stayed in the light grey Ford V-8 with the lights off, as Ed Skogland and J. T. Kearney were closing the safe, and turning off the lights.

The robbers stepped inside as two women customers were leaving, stood at the counter, and asked Kearney for hot chocolate. Then, McKeever walked back into the store, saying, "I see you have quite a store here."

They pulled their guns, and ordered the store owners to "get back and lie on the floor behind the wrapping counter."

"Shell out, you bastard, we know you've got it, and we will get it," McKeever yelled.

He emptied the jewelry safe, and the cash drawer. They frisked the men on the floor, and took their money. When Kearney tried to rise to his elbows, McKeever rushed to him, and acted as if he would kick the prostrate man, but he held back just before making contact with Kearney's face. After about five minutes, the robbers fled with $600 in money and jewelry.

Skogland and Kearney left the store to spread the alarm.[1]

Police circulars were distributed, and pictures of the bandits appeared in local newspapers.

A Shenandoah, Iowa, citizen saw the outlaws, and told the local police where they were hiding.

McKeever, Bostetter, and his wife, were arrested five days later in the late afternoon by Sheriff Keenan and four local police without resistance, as the criminals drove up in a Ford to a house in Shenandoah, where they had taken rooms about a month before. They gave their names as Mr. and Mrs. John Walters, and Frank Nevens of Galesburg, Illinois, and said they were oil salesmen. In their rooms, officers seized a machine gun, a high powered rifle, revolvers, a supply of Ammunition, and a suitcase containing jewelry. Jewelry was also found on the criminals. The Ford carried eight license plates hidden away.

The next day, the two criminals were taken to jail in Clarinda, Iowa, where Sheriff Keenan identified them as Eloy McKeever and Bostetter. They were held for Missouri and Minnesota officers in connection with the murders of Freund, and lawmen Booth and Wilson.

Mrs. Bostetter admitted the two men were Eloy McKeever and Bostetter, and that they had escaped officers in the October gun battle. She, too, was kept at the Shenandoah jail. At the time of the gun battle, officers believed they had flushed out the Pretty Boy Floyd gang.[2]

CHAPTER 14

"I DON'T EVEN KNOW WHAT YOU ARE TALKING ABOUT"

"With these arrests...we are nearing the conclusion in investigation of one of the most troublesome robbery gangs in this part of the country," said Colonel B. Marvin Casteel, director of the Missouri Highway Patrol.[1]

At the Clarinda, Iowa, jail, several Iowa sheriffs asked the two criminals about many robberies. On December 29, 1934, Mover County, Minnesota, Sheriff Ira Syuk, and two of his deputies, left Austin, Minnesota, the county seat, for Clarinda, planning to take back Eloy McKeever and Bostetter for store owner John Freund's murder. Mrs. Bostetter was released that day.[2]

At first, McKeever balked at waiving extradiction, but later consented. The two gangsters were in the Austin jail by December 30. Syck was confident he had a strong case against the pair, and thought McNeiley might be called as a witness.

The next day, McKeever and Bostetter, were in a line-up of seven county jail inmates. Two witnesses identified them as the men who killed Freund. Authorities charged them with first degree murder. Neither of them had thus far admitted to the Johnsburg slaying.

"I don't even know what you are talking about," McKeever insisted.

On the morning of January 2, 1935, the trial began on the charges of first degree murder, with arraignment of the pair before Justice R. L. Stimson, and the drawing of a grand jury of 21 men and women at 11 AM.

The defendants asked for time to reach a decision on whether or not they would demand preliminary hearings. An adjournment was taken until January 11.[3] County Attorney Otto Baudler presented evidence to the jury, and a few witnesses appeared.

Several Iowa officers and robbery victims viewed the gangsters at the Austin jail on January 3. Victims of the Grafton, Iowa, store robbery identified the pair as the holdup men.[4]

The next day, McNeiley and McKeever were officially charged with first degree murder, while Bostetter was charged with second degree murder and grand larceny. McNeiley was held at the Columbia, Missouri, jail.[5]

The prosecution regarded Eloy McKeever as Freund's killer, with Bostetter as the lookout who remained outside in the getaway during the holdup. McKeever lodged a plea of not guilty, as both men were arraigned January 5 in a crowded courtroom before Judge Senn. Bostetter, by his own admission, the lookout in the Johnsburg holdup, did plead guilty to the charge of grand larceny in the second degree, and was sentenced to serve not more than five years at the St. Cloud Reformatory. According to Bostetter, at no time during the robbery did he enter Freund's store, remaining outside in the car.

"I got six or seven dollars of the money taken," he told the court.

Bostetter had difficulty answering the judge as to how many brothers and sisters he had.

He hesitated, finally said "eleven," and declared "four or five" lived in McIntire, Iowa. One brother was serving time at Stillwater, and another at St. Cloud. The 26-year-old defendant said he quit school when he was sixteen-years-old in the 7th grade. He had been married ten months.

Since the defendants had no funds to employ counsel, Judge Senn appointed attorney Marin A. Nelson to represent Bostetter, and Attorney Lafayette French for McKeever. County Attorney, Otto Baudley, represented the State.

Attorney Nelson said, he had advised Bostetter upon hearing the circumstances of the case, the following:

"That it was his duty to himself and society to tell what he knew."

Nelson had no recommendations to make in regard to the impending sentence to be pronounced, but he reminded the Judge that Bostetter had never previously been convicted of a crime.

All the seats in the courtroom were filled, and many spectators stood in the rear of the courtroom. McKeever was not to be brought to trial on the murder charge until the March term of court. Sheriff Syck had Bostetter's confession, and had proof McKeever and McNeiley were in the Johnsburg holdup, which agreed substantially with McNeiley's confession.

Bostetter was sentenced to not more than five years in prison, the maximum penalty for second degree grand larceny. The County Attorney's Office could not ask for a more serious charge, because of the small amount of money involved in the robbery, the fact that Bostetter was believed to be the lookout outside of the store, and not involved in the actual robbery, and Bostetter did not take the money from the holdup victim.[6]

In Sheriff Syuk's custody, Bostetter left for the St. Cloud Reformatory on January 11, 1935. Iowa authorities planned to charge him with other crimes when he was released from prison in five years.[7]

CHAPTER 15

"MY GOD, YOU DON'T THINK I INTENDED TO KILL THAT MAN?"

Eloy McKeever, characterized as "the toughest prisoner ever to be held in jail here," went to trial before Judge Norman E. Peterson on January 18, 1935. McKeever, Bostetter, and McNeiley had all confessed to the sheriff for Freund's murder.[1]

"My God, you don't think I intended to kill that man? If we intended to kill him you don't think we would have left the other man alive?" he said.[2]

The reference to the "other man" was to John Kresback, who was in the store during the murder. McKeever claimed his accomplice, McNeiley, started to struggle with Freund when the latter moved toward the store's side door. The gangster said he went to McNeiley's assistance, and both began striking the storekeeper over the head with their revolvers. He claimed his gun accidentally discharged.[3]

"I shot once. It was an accidental shot. Freund was wrestling with McNeiley, and I went to help, and the gun went off accidentally."[4]

The confession that morning broke a reticence that McKeever had maintained since his arrest in Shenandoah, Iowa, on December 17. He had first consulted his attorney, Lafayette French, and then gave his confession to the Sheriff. Prior to this, McKeever's answer to questions about the crime was usually: "I don't even know what you're talking about."[5]

Attorney French told the court, While it was not his purpose to minimize the taking of a human life, the greater portion of McKeever's life had not been spent in crime, but as a mechanic.

On the night in question, it was McNeiley who placed the gun against Freund to hold him up. It is quite apparent that Mr. Freund became frightened, lost his head, and attempted to fight with McNeiley. In the course of the struggle, the gun was discharged. There is this to the credit of McKeever, that he, at least, was not a professional killer of the gangster type. Or Kresback would not have been left alive. It is quite apparent to me that the offense would have been robbery only if it had not been for the struggle of Freund to get away from McNeiley. I know the life sentence is mandatory.[6]

John Kresback, a witness to the slaying, told the court otherwise. He said both bandits were striking Freund with guns when McNeiley said to McKeever:

"Plug him."

"McKeever stepped back, held out his gun, and shot Freund," Kresback said.[7]

The witness held his arm out straight to show the court how McKeever pointed the gun toward Freund to fire the fatal shot. The Sheriff produced a German Luger pistol, which McKeever identified as the weapon with which he shot Freund in the holdup.

On that day, McKeever insisted Bostetter entered the Johnsburg store after the shooting, and took two cartons of cigarettes. Bostetter had said he had not entered the store earlier, and at no time during the holdup did he enter the Johnsburg store.

Sheriff Syck stated McKeever's story would be investigated, and, if it was found Bostetter did enter the store, he would very likely be brought back to face a more serious charge. He told the court that, until McKeever had confessed on January 18, the authorities did not know Bostetter had entered the store during the holdup. According to McKeever, both Freund and Kresback were lying on the floor when Bostetter entered.[8]

"Imprisonment at hard labor in the Stillwater Penitentiary for the period of your natural life," was the sentence Judge Peterson gave McKeever, on the late afternoon of January 18.[9]

McKeever was not nervous, and he maintained his composure as he heard his sentence pronounced. It was not until he returned to the county jail that he displayed signs of being upset. During the next few days, he became visibly downhearted and asked numerous questions about life in the state penitentiary.[10] McKeever's wife, Anne, visited him at the Austin, Minnesota, jail, before he went to Stillwater prison on January 20, 1935. Anne brought cigars and candy, and told him she would "wait for him."[11] The well-dressed McKeever left the Austin jail in low spirits on the morning of January 22, as he set out with Sheriff Syck for the penitentiary.[12]

CHAPTER 16

TEN MORE YEARS

Bostetter had to face trial for Freund's murder in the Mower County, Minnesota, court. He was returned from the St. Cloud Reformatory on March 13, 1935. Martin A. Nelson, Bostetter's lawyer, was reappointed to represent him

Bostetter appeared that day in court, guarded by two reformatory guards, who were told to let him consult with Nelson and, then, to take him back to St. Cloud. They were to produce him in court again four days later. Previously, the court believed the criminal had been the lookout, and had not entered the Johnsburg store during the robbery and murder. County Attorney, A. C. Richardson, asked for a new day in court, because Bostter's participation in a felony that resulted in a murder made him an accomplice in the greater crime.[1]

Bostetter told the judge he wished to withdraw his plea of not guilty to the murder degree, on which he was indicted, and enter a plea of guilty to manslaughter. He took the witness stand and was asked by the judge if he had planned the store robbery with McKeever and McNeiley.

"I couldn't say they went in the store to rob. I thought they went in to get some beer," he replied.

"Why did you remain outside the store?" was the next question.

"I guess I was just slow in starting to go into the store," he replied.

"You claim then that you were a perfectly innocent bystander," the judge asked.

"Yes," Bostetter replied.

However, the Judge was not able to accept the defendant's plea of guilty to manslaughter.[2]

The next morning, Bostetter again told the lie that he had not planned to rob the store. However, that afternoon, the criminal refuted the story he had told that morning and admitted he had helped to plan the store robbery with his two companions, then gone there to carry the plans out. Then, his plea of manslaughter was accepted. He was sentenced to no more than fifteen years at the St. Cloud Reformatory.[3]

Twelve people were named to share in the five hundred dollar reward offered by the Mower County, Minnesota, board for the arrest of the three bandits who had killed Freund. Sheriff Syck recommended that John Kresback, who had been at the murder scene, should get $125.[4]

CHAPTER 17

"I AM READY TO PAY"

Pretty Boy Floyd and Adam Richetti, whom everyone believed had carried out the McKeever gang's murders and robberies, were cleared of the murders of the lawmen Booth and Wilson on November 28, 1934, after McNelley had been arrested for these murders three days earlier.[1]

George McKeever was taken from the North Dakota Penitentiary on January 2, 1935, by Missouri officers. They took him by car to the Columbia, Missouri, jail; arriving the next day. He denied he had killed anyone and plead not guilty.[2]

The evidence against McKeever was very strong, such as McNeiley's voluntary statement made on December 18, 1934. There also was the ballistics evidence from Kansas City ballistics expert, Merle Gill, that showed a match between the .45-caliber bullet in Booth's leg and the .45-caliber gun found in McNeiley's possession. Boone County, Missouri, County Attorney, W. H. Sapp, said the State had clear cases against both McKeever and McNeiley, and the two would be given an immediate trial.

"McNeiley has signed a written confession of his part in the crime, implicating George McKeever," Sapp said. "Ballistics tests prove that the bullets that killed Sergeant Booth were fired from a gun owned and used by George McKeever at the time of the slaying."

McNeiley had told officers it was his brother-in-law George McKeever's gun, and that he had lied at first because he disliked Eloy McKeever for mistreating his sister Anne and wanted him punished for the murders. He also was upset over the division of money from a bank robbery.[3]

McKeever's preliminary hearing was held on January 12.[4]

Two days later, McNeiley plead guilty in Columbia, Missouri, to first degree murder in the killing of Sheriff Roger Wilson. Sentence was deferred by Judge W. M. Dinwiddle. Defense counsel had requested time to obtain affidavits concerning McNeiley's character from people near Clarinda, Iowa, the gangster's hometown. Sentence then would not be given until completion of George McKeever's trial. McNeiley was to be a prosecution witness.[5]

"Whatever debt society thinks I owe," McNelley said, "I am ready to pay. Nobody else can pay for me."[6]

At a hearing on January 15, George McKeever was turned over to the Boone County, Missouri, Circuit Court on a charge of murder for the slaying of Sergeant Booth. McNeiley appeared as a witness for the state and described how George McKeever shot Booth during the struggle with the officer.

A dramatic part of the hearing was when McKeever cross-examined McNeiley.

"When you were first arrested you said my brother, Eloy McKeever, was with you, didn't you."

"Sure," returned McNeiley.

"And now you say I was with you."

"Yes."

"What was the reason for that?" George McKeever asked.

McNeiley answered he was trying to protect his friend.

"Why do you now say it was I who was with you?"

"Because it leaked out anyway," McNeiley explained.[7]

George McKeever was arraigned January 26 on a first degree murder charge in the killing of Sergeant Ben Booth. Todd Gentry, former North Dakota Attorney General and Supreme Court Justice, and George F. Hollis were appointed attorneys for McKeever when he said he had no money to provide counsel.[8]

Gentry contended McKeever's preliminary hearing at Columbia January 12 was illegal because the defendant was not given sufficient time to obtain counsel and get witnesses. On this basis, Defense Counsel refused to enter a plea at McKeever's arraignment in court on February 4. Judge Dinwiddle overruled a motion by Gentry to quash the indictment. The court entered a plea of not guilty for the defendant and set March 18 as the trial date.

"I asked McKeever if he was represented and told him I would give him time to secure one," Byars testified, "but he said he was ready to plead, and he pleaded not guilty."

"Did the defendant at either the preliminary or the arraignment request the appointment of an attorney?" Judge Dinwiddle asked.

Byars said he had not. The court remarked, "The evidence doesn't show the defendant was pushed through the preliminary" in overruling the motion to quash the indictment.

McNeiley agreed to testify against McKeever, while McKeever repeatedly denied he had killed anyone."[9]

McKeever's relatives were called to testify at his March 18 trial, but his counsel wanted a change of venue to Fulton, Missouri, later approved. Anne McKeever, Eloy McKeever's wife, Mrs. Mary Gannon, the widowed sister of George McKeever, and McNeiley's brother Barge were subpoenaed. Mrs. Gannon was recently reported to be hitch-hiking through Missouri in a search for evidence that would help her brother's defense.[10]

Since George McKeever looked like Pretty Boy Floyd, Missouri Highway Patrol Major Lewis Means began a search of small banks that were believed to have been robbed by him.

One of the banks was in Gretna, Nebraska. Bank President E. H. Stelling and the bank's cashier identified pictures of George McKeever as one of the men who had robbed them of cash and had taken Stelling's pistol. Stelling did not know if the gun taken from McNeiley was his.

Moveover, he told Means that once, many years ago, he had accidently fired it at the Gretna bank's floor. Means and Stelling went to the bank, which had been closed after its robbery, and made a careful search for the bullet.[11]

According to one writer:

Major Means and Stelling went to the building and with the permission of the owner unlocked the doors. The rusty hinges squeaked and rattled as the pair entered. A small hole in the wooden floor where Stelling's office had been was covered with tin to keep out insects and rodents. This was removed and Major Means began a careful procedure to recover the bullet. The angle of entrance through the floor was estimated and a long piece of heavy wire was inserted at the approximate line of slight. The wire was pushed about five feet into the ground and the work of seeking the bullet began. Major Means carefully sifted each shovel full of earth that came from a five- foot circle around the wire. Four feet from the surface of the ground, the search was rewarded by the bullet.[12]

After finding the bullet, they send it to ballistics expert, Merle Gill, who found that the bullet matched the bullet from lawman Benjamin Booth's leg; it was from Stelling's gun.[13]

CHAPTER 18

"AN ENDEAVOR TO PREJUDICE THE JURORS AND SPECTATORS"

Just before 9 P M on June 12, 1935, George McKeever and McNeiley were taken into the Callaway County, Missouri, Circuit Court courtroom, and their handcuffs were removed. The room was jammed with officers. There had been a change of venue to Fulton, Missouri.

McKeever did not talk to anyone other than his attorneys. Smiling, McNeiley was talking with court officers, but there was a "marked nervousness" in his manner.

Alice Booth, widow of murdered patrolman Benjamin Booth, her two small children, her father, and Major Means took seats in the courtroom.

The State had subpoenaed sixty witnesses, including ballistic expert, Merle Gill; Anne McKeever, wife of Eloy McKeever; Barge McNeiley, brother of Francis McNeiley; and Albert R. Stelling, an eyewitness to one of George McKeever's bank robberies.[1]

At 1:30 PM, the trial of George McKeever began with the selection of a jury. McKeever was kept in the Columbia jail because the

Fulton jail was in poor condition. Transportation to and from the Fulton courthouse was handled by the Missouri State Patrol.

Judge W. D. Dinwiddle appointed Judge N. T. Gentry, and George S. Hollis to represent the defendant. The State's side of the case was presented by W. H. Sapp and T. A. Fauceit, the Prosecuting Attorneys of Boone and Callaway Counties respectively.

The entire morning was spent considering motions of the defense attorneys, each motion of which Judge Dinwiddle denied. The lawyers made a motion that the Prosecuting Attorney and all others who had confessions and affidavits relating to this case had to turn them over to the defense. Gentry argued the papers should be given to them as fair play. Prosecutor Sapp had, before George McKeever's arrest, charged Adam Richetti with the murder of Ben Booth. Some witnesses, who were going to be called in the present trial, had identified Richetti as the man who killed Booth.

Gentry filed a motion that charged that the large number of State Patrolmen had used their weapons "in an endeavor to prejudice the jurors and spectators." Judge Dinwiddle overruled the motion.

A motion for a new trial had not been written, so it was necessary to recess court for an hour while the motion was prepared. The Defense Attorneys replied they were not ready for trial, and asked for a continuance on the ground of two missing "material" witnesses. The motion noted that Eloy McKeever, in a Minnesota prison, had certain testimony he would give if he were in court. His deposition had not been taken. Until the last few days the evidence he could give was unknown to the counsels.

The second material witness not in Fulton was Robert Hicks of Carbondale, Illinois. George McKeever's wife and sister had met this man while hitchhiking in Illinois the previous day. He told them he had been at the crime scene and been shown pictures of McKeever and McNeiley. While he recognized McNeiley as one of the Columbia murderers, he was sure McKeever was not there. Judge Dinwiddle considered this motion, and, as it was 11:30 AM, he recessed the Court until 1:15 PM. The court session ended at 3 PM. Jurors were to be chosen the following morning at 9:30, whereupon they would start taking evidence.[2]

CHAPTER 19

"THIS IS A HIGHWAY PATROL CASE"

On June 13, 1935, following jury selection, a heated argument ensued between Defense Counsels, Gentry and Hollis, and Prosecutors Sepp and Faurett over the defense demand for the confessions and affidavits held by the State. For example, they demanded the confessions signed by McNeiley, where he said he and Eloy McKeever killed the two police officers.

Gentry also wanted to get the depositions the Missouri State Patrol filled out regarding taking Adam Richetti to the Columbia, Missouri jail. Judge Dinwiddle overruled the defense motion.

Prosecutor Sapp made the opening statement for the State. He proclaimed he would have many witnesses and would describe in great detail the events before, during, and after the murders.[1]

"When McNeiley was arrested in Iowa he had the .45 pistol, which he said belonged to George McKeever. This gun had been stolen from a Grenta, Nebraska, bank which had been robbed by McKeever and others," he said.

Sapp continued, "A ballistic expert of Kansas City will testify that this .45 is the gun which fired the bullet that struck Ben Booth in the leg. Eyewitnesses of the shooting will identify both men."[2]

Gentry briefly spoke on future defense testimony. He described the sensation when the murderers were falsely reported to have been in a cornfield in south Callaway County, Missouri.

"They were just as certain then they had their men located as they are certain now that they have the right men," Sapp said.[3]

McKeever's lawyer complained about the confession McNeiley gave the officers when he was first arrested.

"In that confession he said he and Eloy McKeever did the shooting, and the Prosecuting Attorney now has it in his possession, but will not turn it over to us!" Gentry shouted.[4]

McNeiley then changed his confession and named George instead of Eloy.

To a reporter, Gentry said, "McNeiley explained his naming of Eloy in the first instance because Eloy had mistreated his sister and he hated Eloy."

"McNeiley pleaded guilty to the murder of Sheriff Wilson at the January term of the Circuit Court. That term of Court is gone, and the April term has also come and gone, but he has not been sentenced," declared Gentry.

He charged it had been arranged with the State Patrol that1 he would receive a lighter sentence if he testified against George McKeever.

"This is a Highway Patrol case," he insisted.

McNeiley's appearance in Court, "all nicely dressed," was by the State Patrol, Gentry believed.

"He has been the star boarder of the Boone County Jail since he made the confession." [5]

Testimony began when Boone County, Missouri, highway engineer, D. E. Hill, presented a drawing that showed the intersection where the shooting occurred, Highway 63 and 40 at Columbia, Missouri. When he took the stand as the next witness, J. H. Wally, reporter-photographer of the *Columbia Missourian*, identified pictures he took of that intersection.

Mrs. Dorothy Schubert and her 15-year-old nephew, both of St. Louis, said they had known McNeiley for about five years. She, George McKeever, and McNeiley, spent the night of June 15, 1933, in her rooming house, the day after the murders of Booth and Wilson.

Albert R. Stelling, who had once worked at a Gretna, Nebraska, bank, gave testimony about a revolver that had been stolen from a drawer immediately under the cashier's window. Supposedly, the gun was later used to fire a bullet into patrolman Booth's left leg.

Stelling also testified he made a trip to the Columbia, Missouri, jail, in April 1935, to identify George McKeever as the man he saw in his bank's robbery. [6]

Missouri University pathologist Dr. C. C. Pflaum, who had performed autopsies on the bodies of Booth and Wilson, took the witness stand in the afternoon.

"I have performed 700 autopsies," he testified in qualifying as an expert.

Pflaum did admit he knew nothing of ballistics, and went into detail on the nature of the wounds.[7]

The next witness was Robert Brock of Kansas City, the manager of the All-States Hotel and Cabins, who was an eyewitness to the murders, and probably the closest witness. He was on a lawn about 100 feet from the scene of the tragedy. It had been a bright afternoon between 2 PM and 3 PM, and he had a clear view of the event. As he heard the first shot, he looked in that direction and saw Booth with a man caught by the wrists. Booth's right hand was on the man's right hand, in which there was a gun, and his left hand on the man's left wrist.

Booth pulled the man from the Ford coupe, and Booth fell down, with the patrolman underneath the man. As the murderer jerked his hand loose and fired, Booth's hold relaxed.

Asked if he could identify George McKeever as the man who shot Booth, Brock said, The features very strikingly resembled that man. I am almost positive he (pointing to McKeever) is the man. Booth's killer had long, black hair, and his beard was dark. He was wearing a cap, white shirt and dark pants.[8]

This description was like that of McKeever, as he sat next to his attorney.

Brock also told of the murder of Sheriff Wilson, saying he saw a man in a car shoot at the Sheriff. But he could not identity McNeiley as that man.[9]

Automobile salesman, Sam Baruck, the next witness, testified McNeiley was the same man who called himself "Joe Clark," when he bought an used car from him for $20 in St. Louis in April 1933.[10]

The final witness of the day was ballistic expert, Merle Gill, who testified that the revolver stolen from a Gretna, Nebraska bank was used in the murders. According to him, a bullet, which had lodged in the left ankle of Patrolman Ben Booth, was discharged from that gun. Gill had with him two enlarged pictures that showed a small part of the bullet that had been taken from Booth's leg and a bullet from the Gretna Bank gun. He also had two enlarged pictures of the bullet from Booth and a test shot he had fired in his experimental laboratory.

Those who saw the photos were convinced they were accurate.

The ballistic expert stated he had been a firearms identification expert for the past eight years, that he had made 191 courtroom appearances, and that, in the past seven years, he had made thousands of test shot identifications. He had examined the bullets of the Barrow Gang, of Pretty Boy Floyd, of Adam Richetti, and many gangster guns from Kansas City and St. Louis in his search to find the one that matched the bullet taken from patrolman Booth's leg. It was only from the gun found on McNeiley.[11]

CHAPTER 20

"I EXPECT TO GET THE SUPREME PENALTY"

In a calm, low voice, with solemn demeanor, on June 14, 1935, McNeiley went to the witness stand at 9:30 AM to give evidence against his brother-in-law, George McKeever. He seemed to be a thoughtful man telling the truth. The gangster went into great detail about the events of June 14, 1933, the day when the two lawmen were murdered.

Two confessions signed by McNeiley were introduced in court. In the first confession, he said Eloy McKeever was his partner in the June 1933 murders; but, in the second, he insisted George McKeever killed Ben Booth.

Prosecutor Sapp asked McNeiley if he had signed any statements about the murders. He replied he had, whereupon they introduced his two signed confessions into evidence. The Defense Attorneys, who had been asking for these confessions, finally received them.

They asked McNeiley about his guilty plea and whether his sentence was deferred.

"That was correct," McNeiley replied.

"Do you expect a lighter sentence for pleading guilty," they asked him.

"No sir," he said,

"What sentence do you expect?"

"I expect to get the supreme penalty," he calmly answered.

The lawyers described the trips McNeiley made to and from Columbia, which were always with Sapp and state patrol officers. He was asked why he was so eager to help Sapp during the trial.

"It was my duty to society," McNeiley replied.

"Did you think you were doing a duty to society when you killed the Sheriff?"

McNeiley did not answer.

"I did not know Pretty Boy Floyd or Adam Richetti," he said.

The gangster denied he had told George McKeever's mother he and Eloy had killed the two officers.

McNeiley insisted the clothes he was wearing at the trial belonged to him before the trial and that state patrolmen had never given him anything or did any favors for him.

"I told newspaper reporters Eloy McKeever knew no principles and was unkind to all his family," McNeiley said.

"Whereas George McKeever," he continued, "was always good to his mother, and that was the reason I tried to shield George. I always admired him for that," McNeiley said.

McNeiley gave only a fair performance during his cross-examination by Defense Attorneys, Gentry and Hollis. Some of his statements were difficult to believe. It was generally believed that he made a good witness for the State, and the Defense Attorneys were unable to make him contradict his testimony.[1]

Five eyewitnesses to the murders testified; "They differed in some particulars concerning what had happened; but, in the main, told the same stories as the witnesses who had preceded them," indicated a newspaper account.

Only plumber, Arley Houcke, who was at work on the house on the corner, only 28 steps from the getaway car during the murders, was at variance over the number of shots fired and who fired them. He insisted only one man shot at Booth, and that he used the same gun when he fired five times.

Mr. and Mrs. Ed Gurdes of Harviell, Missouri, whose farm McKeever and McNeily lived on during early 1933, also testified. They did not like McKeever.[2]

CHAPTER 21

"WE ACCESS THE PUNISHMENT
AT DEATH"

On June 15, 1935, George McKeever sat slumped in a chair in the courtroom, while his heavily-guarded brother-in-law, McNeiley, was on the other side of the room. Both were expressionless.[1]

According to a newspaper account:

The strain of the trial is plainly showing in McKeever and McNeiley. Both looked haggard as they appeared in court Saturday morning. McKeever, who had been rather relaxed during the recital of witnesses, appeared tense and on a strain. He sat with his hands clinched across his body and kept a keen eye on everything that was happening. McNeiley rested his head in his hands, his eyes downcast.[2]

Anne McKeever testified that morning that her husband, Eloy, was with her from June 8 to June 22, 1933, at Keokik, Iowa, and could not have been near Columbia at the time of the slayings on June 14.

Berg McNeiley discribed seeing his brother Francis with George McKeever in a car answering to the description of the killers' vehicle.

Major Lewis Means of the Missouri Highway Patrol, the last witness for the State, appeared at 11 AM. He described the details of the case and identified guns and bullets already introduced as State exhibits. There had been forty-six witnesses for the State.[3]

Chief witnesses for the Defense were Mrs. Lucy Clark, and newspaper reporter, L. Hollis Edwards, of Columbia. Mrs. Clark testified she was unable to identify either killer, and had tentatively identified a picture of Pretty Boy Floyd as one of the slayers.

Edwards reported he had obtained an interview with McNeiley at the Columbia, Missouri, jail on why McNeiley named Eloy McKeever, instead of George McKeever as his companion in the killings.

"He said he first named Eloy because Eloy was cruel to his sister," Edwards stated.

The Defense closed its case in the late afternoon.[4]

The jury began deliberation about 7:30 PM. McKeever talked with reporter, J. H. Wally, of the *Columbia Missourian* as the jury deliberated on McKeever's fate. Wally wrote:

I sat and talked with George McKeever at his request from the time his fate was put in the hands of the jury Saturday night until it returned an hour and an half later with a death verdict. The man, now convicted of having blown out the life of Sergt. Ben Booth's prone body here two years ago, called me from across the courtroom...A half- dozen uniformed highway patrolmen watched me closely as I sat beside him. Then the man...asked:

"How was that big picture made?"

He referred to State Exhibit B, a giant three-foot photo of the intersection where the two officers fell under flashing guns. Evidently, it had aroused his curiosity, as he listened intently to the answer.

"All in one piece?" he queried.

Leaning back at the affirmative reply, George lit a cigarette. His black eyes flashed and he smiled out the corner of his mouth. Shortly, he leaned forward and asked another question.

"They didn't prove me guilty, did they?"

I assured him it was all a matter of opinion. I believed him guilty, but could not help telling him how a Callaway County jury had reduced Floyd Brown's murder sentence from fifty to ten years in 1933. He replied that he never had heard the name Floyd Brown...

"There was a pause after he asked my age," I told him.

"I thought you were older than that," he laughed.

"Not very complimentary of me, is it..."

"You don't seem very worried, George."

He passed the statement off as if I had never spoken, saying, "Some jury, huh?...Just like a b unch of wooden Indians."

The conversion got around to the recent Baer-Braddock fisticuffs.

George said he couldn't figure that fight at all, and he 'sure like to get hold of a blow-by-blow account.'

He called attention to the fact that he had done a little boxing himself while in the Marine Corps in 1920-21. He claimed six fights in the service, and one at the White City Chicago Amusement Center...His part of the purse was $8, of which $2.70 went to his 'second.' The fight ended in a draw.

"Never could understand what the seventy cents went for," he laughed, shaking all over.

George follows horse racing news regularly. He professed the opinion that it is 'foolish for anybody to put money on a filly,' mentioning one of the leading contemporary horses...and 'it pays to put your money on the other kind.'"[5]

After fewer than two hours deliberation, the jury found McKeever guilty in the first degree and assessed the death penalty for punishment. Just before 10 PM the foreman gave Judge Dinwiddle the verdict.[6]

The jury wrote, "We, the jury, find the defendant guilty of murder in the first degree, as charged, and assess the punishment at death."[7]

It was the first time since the Civil War that either a jury or judge in Callaway Country had assessed the death penalty. As he heard himself condemned to death, McKeever calmly chewed a huge wad of gum, lit a cigarette, and shrugged his shoulders. Wearing a half smile, he ignored press requests for a statement.

"Sorry, fellow, but I can't do a thing for you."[8]

Arrangements were made that night to send him to prison. As he walked by the press Table, he smiled sadly. His attorneys were given until June 24, 1935, to file a motion for a new trial.[9]

At 10:55 AM on June 18, McNeiley was sentenced by Judge Dinwiddle to life imprisonment. The gangster, handcuffs removed, calmly accepted the sentence.[10]

McNeiley asked if there were any questions reporters would like to ask him:

I think I've been shown the greatest consideration. The officers, the Sheriff and the State patrolmen have treated me with the greatest consideration and respect they could within their rights and while in charge of a person accused of an offense such as mine. I have no grudge or ill-feeling against anyone in the court or against any of the officers with whom I've had contact. I realized who and what they are and what their duties to society are. I have no criticism to make of the whole thing.

I told the truth to the best of my ability as saw it and as I can remember it...There was no detail exaggerated or omitted.[11]

McNeiley believed them to be some of the greatest men he had known. Major Means he described as "one of the finest men ever to wear a uniform," and praised the good treatment the state highway patrol had given him throughout. When asked what he thought about George and Eloy McKeever, McNeiley, with a cigarette in his mouth, said, "I have no grudge against either George or Eloy. I have no grudge against anyone."

The prisoner stood up and extended his wrists, so handcuffs could be put on him.

McNeiley turned, walked out of the courtroom at 2:25 PM, and was taken to his cell. When he was leaving the jail to go to the state penitentiary, he smiled, and waved good bye.[12]

The *Jefferson City* MO *Post-Tribune* reported:

Francis McNeiley saved his neck by squealing on a confederate. But is he fortunate?

For George McKeever it will soon be over while McNeiley, 23 years old, has a life-time behind old gray walls, his dreams full of visions not only of the slain officer but a pal mounting the gallows, sent there by his testimony.[13]

CHAPTER 22

"THE BLOODIEST FORTY-SEVEN
ACRES IN AMERICA"

The Missouri State Penitentiary, the first prison to be built west of the Mississippi, was one of the oldest and largest prisons in the United States. The only prison in the state, it was on the Missouri River bluffs just seven blocks east of the state capitol in Jefferson City. Opened on four acres in 1836, it could house only forty prisoners. By 1836, the prison's overcrowding meant two men was put in cells first built for one. In the 1900s, the prison was called "the bloodiest forty-seven acres in America." Tough discipline was practiced. Whipping, the ball and chain, cold baths, and the sweatbox were common punishments. There was little inmnate education. Guards, who were political hires, had a high turnover rate, received low pay and had little training.

In 1918, the State Prison Board, influenced by progressive beliefs, took over control of the prison. Among its many reforms were that prisoners were given wages, inmates earned time off under the 5/12 rule (five months off for good behavior for every year of the sentence); the horrible punishment of the "rings"—being suspended for a long time—was eliminated; the Office of Warden was no longer a political appointment; and they added a few programs to help prisoners reform.

One year later, two prisoners, Kate Richards O'Hare and Emma Goldman, were sent to "Jeff City" for anti-war activities. They were frequent critics of prisons, writing about the unsanitary conditions and the use of "slave labor." Their reports appeared in newspapers and magazines, and they wrote to State Legislators and Congressmen.

The inmates still had twelve hour jobs and such punishments as flogging. As before, all inmates had to walk in lockstep to and from work and meals. Still, there were too few guards and not enough rehabilitation programs. The food service and medical care were poor. There was too much drug trade, inmate violence, and gang warfare.

The prison remained a human warehouse, with the number of inmates increasing at a high rate. In 1913, there were about 2500 prisoners. Twelve years later, there were 500 more.

In 1929, the prison housed about 4000 inmates, about 80 percent over official capacity. Blacks, who endured the worst overcrowding, lived in one building—"A Hall"—where seven or eight men were crowded into cells supposed to be for three. Women had a separate building.

From the 1880s to the 1930s, the prison was as much a business operation as it was a prison. Labor for profit was the main goal. The Superintendent of Industries made more money than the Warden. Although farmers purchased prison products at very low prices, the state made huge profits from it because little was spent feeding and clothing prisoners. Prison factories made shoes, work clothing, and binding twine, as well as soap, gloves, and furniture.

The vehicle-tag plant made State license tags and highway signs. In 1923, the Warden's biennial report stated, "Healthy and proper rivalry obtains among the different factories as to which can best serve the State." By 1925 the prison was making about five million dollars a year in profits.[1]

CHAPTER 23

"MCKEEVER MUST PAY FOR MURDER

WITH HIS LIFE"

George McKeever sat alone in the Missouri State Penitentiary in a small death row cell in the basement of one of the cell blocks, waiting for an appeal to the Missouri Supreme Court on his fate. Conditions were bad. There was no contact with other prisoners. Natural light did not exist, and, sometimes his cell flooded. His only exercise out of his cell was for forty-five minutes three times a week. He only got two meals a day.[1]

Before the June 24, 1935, appeal deadline, McKeever's lawyers filed a three-part motion to the Callaway County, Missouri, Circuit Court for a new trial. His lawyers claimed there was a prejudicial error committed by the Court, when several Missouri Highway Patrol members, in full uniform with guns in their belts in public view, appeared during the trial over the repeated objections of his attorneys.

The lawyers also insisted that having the defendants brought in and out of the courtroom handcuffed and in the custody of state highway patrolmen instead of deputy sheriffs was a p rejudicial error. The highway patrolmen, it was claimed, were not appointed Deputy Sheriffs, and were not approved by the Court.

The third claim was that Merle Gill, the Kansas City gun expert, was not qualified to testify a bullet fired out of a pistol and buried in the ground for ten years was similar to the bullet found in Booth's body, as well as, and that both bullets were fired by McKeever's .45 automatic pistol.[2]

On July 13, 1935, McKeever was formally sentenced to be hanged at Fulton, Missouri, on September 6, 1935. After his motions had been denied, McKeever's lawyer immediately filed an appeal that would be taken to the Missouri Supreme Court. The appeal automatically set aside McKeever's execution date, pending decision by the State High Tribunal.[3]

On August 19, 1935, out of respect to the first Missouri State Trooper to fall in the line of duty. Missori Highway Patrol Superintendant, Colonel B. M. Casteel, ordered Ben Booth's patrol shield no. 13 remain blank on the Roll.[4]

One month later, on September 26, reporter, H. W. Brown, interviewed McNeiley's sister,

Anne McKeever, "She sought love, but found in marriage death, jail, and disgrace for her husband, brother, and brother-in-law instead..."

Anne said, "I don't blame Eloy. I don't blame George. I don't have a grudge against any of them. I think Francis was brave to confess. It was just as he said: He wanted to do his duty to society... Francis is a good boy."[5]

On November 17, 1935, the Missouri Supreme Court ruled "McKeever must pay for murder with his life at Fulton, Missouri, on December 18, 1936."

Only a reprieve or a commutation of sentence from Governor Guy B. Park would save McKeever from being hanged, unless the Missouri Supreme Court would agree to rehear the case.

In appealing to the Missouri Supreme Court, Counsel for McKeever claimed McNeiley was "unworthy of belief." However, "The conviction does not hinge on the testimony of McNeiley," the Court held in an opinion written by Commissioner Walter H. Bohling.

"Eyewitnesses, other than McNeiley, to the homicide," it added, "positively identified McKeever, as well as McNeiley, and testified McKeever was the man struggling with Sergeant Booth and the man who fired the fatal shot into his body."[6]

Two of the three convicted Missouri murderers were held in the Missouri State Penitentiary under a smallpox and typhoid fever quarantine in November 1936. However, Warden J. M. Sanders said the quarantine would not interfere with returning the two, McKeever and Fred Adams, to the counties where they were convicted and sentenced to hang,"[7]

There was almost no news about McKeever during most of 1936, but he was reported to have been in fair mental and physical health.[8]

CHAPTER 24

"RECONCILED TO HIS FATE"

On November 27, 1936, George McKeever's attorneys asked the State Supreme Court to rehear his appeal. After the motion was denied by the Court on December 9, his execution seemed certain.[1] It was rumored the Governor would not interfere in the Court's findings.

On December 14, Governor Park indicated he would not grant a stay of execution.

McKeever's mother, his wife, Pearl, and several others wrote to the Governor seeking a stay of execution or commutation of sentence. His mother requested her son's sentence be commuted to life imprisonment. They believed McKeever did not kill the state patrolmen.

Warden J. M. Sanders allowed family members to visit McKeever, but did not commute his sentence.[2]

George P. Hollis, McKeever's counsel, visited him at the penitentiary on Sunday afternoon, December 13. The gangster still said he was not guilty, and Hollis thought McNeiley should tell the officers he did not kill Sergeant Booth.[3]

Boone County, Missouri, County Prosecuting Attorney, W. H. Sapp, and Sheriff Pleas Wright were in Fulton on the afternoon of December 14 conferring with Callaway County,

Missouri, Prosecuting Attorney, Ancel Faucett, and Sheriff Harris Wells on arrangements for the execution. Sapp thought it unusual, but the McKeever case was really their case. Boone County Officers were to help Callaway County officers with the execution.[4]

McKeever's gray-haired mother, Clara B. McKeever, and his wife, Pearl, left their home in Burlington, Iowa, on December 15 for Jefferson City. The Governor, after a fifteen minute conference with the two women the next day, remarked he would "look into the case further" and instructed his secretary to get him the complete case file for study.

The women told the Governor they were confident McKeever did not kill Booth. They had evidence to prove he was not at the crime scene. On December 16 the women returned.[5]

McKeever's lawyer, Hollis, accompanied an eyewitness to the murders of Booth and Wilson, A. "Al" Nichols, to Jefferson City on the afternoon of December 16. After seeing McKeever at the penitentiary, the two men conferred with Governor Park. Nichols, an eyewitness to the two murders at Columbia, had remained silent as to what he had seen and did not testify at McKeever's trial. After discussing the matter with friends, Nichols contacted Hollis. Hearing about Nichols, the attorney believed his story might result in McKeever's reprieve.

The Governor met with Nichol, but found nothing convincing. Nichols told the Governor he was at a gas station at the junction of highways 40 and 63, where the killing took place. He heard shots, looked out of his car, and saw the murders being committed about 90 feet away. He then stepped behind a gasoline pump. Nichols insisted "a short stubby" man, who did not fit McKeever's description, was one of the killers. He did recognize McNeiley as the other killer.

After talking with Nichols, Governor Park remarked that the Missouri Supreme Court, in upholding the death penalty, had pointed out the evidence showed that no other verdict could have been made. He had no doubt in his mind as to McKeever's guilt.

Having reviewed the trial record against McKeever and the Missouri Supreme Court opinion, he believed Nichols was "sincere in his beliefs," but was confused. Hollis conferred with the Governor, but no legal action was taken to stop the execution.[6]

The condemned man appeared on December 16 to await death, with the same outward calm he had displayed at his June 1935 trial. Missouri Highway Patrol Director Casteel said a recent visit with McKeever at the prison had convinced him the doomed man had accepted his fate.

"Oh, I'm as well as could be expected," the Highway Patrol head quoted him as saying.[7]

Work on the scaffold McKeever would hang on, continued in the old barn at the rear of the jail. It was Callaway County's first hanging since a black woman slave was executed in 1856.

The wooden scaffold was built at the left side of the barn, and the west side of the barn was removed to permit those in the enclosure to see the execution and make room for more witnesses. Canvass was stretched from the north and south corners on the jail's east side. An awning was placed on the west gable to hide the execution from public view, as the law required the execution take place within an enclosure.[8]

Sheriff Wells issued three hundred invitations to officers, newspaper reporters and others to witness the execution. Included among these were fifty Missouri State Highway patrol members. Several invitations were sent to Boone County, Missouri, Sheriff Pleas Wright, and Columbia, Missouri, Chief of Police, O. H. Pollock.

The invitation read:

You are invited to attend the execution of George McKeever on Friday, December 18,

1936, at 7:30 a. m. at the County Jail in Fulton, Missouri.
HARRIS WELLS, Sheriff
Please present this card at entrance.[9]

Sergeant Ben Booth's wife, Sally, requested and was given four invitations to the execution. Her request that her two minor children, 11 and 12, be allowed witness the execution was denied. The wife of the slain Sheriff, Roger Wilson, at first declined invitations to witness the execution, but later changed her mind.[10]

"McKeever appeared to be reconciled to his fate," Warden J. M. Sanders said.

Meanwhile, McKeever prepared to go to the gallows as the last hope for a stay vanished, with word from the Governor that "my present intention is not to grant a reprieve."

Prosecuting Attorney Sapp said that morning he had no desire to witness the hanging.

On December 17, the night before his execution, McKeever had a chicken dinner as his last dinner. Sheriff Wells announced the last details for the execution were done. The noose was tied and tried, with a 200 pound sand bag dropped though the trap. The scaffold was also tested.

The Missouri State Highway Patrol took McKeever to the Fulton jail late in the afternoon.

Outward calm that characterized McKeever at his 1935 trial, and later as he carried his fight for his life to the State Supreme Court, vanished as he paced back and forth in his small jail cell.

"We intend to take every precaution right up to the end," Colonel Casteel said on December 17. "McKeever will be heavily guarded from the time he is turned over to us until he walks up the scaffold."[11]

CHAPTER 25

"I FEEL JUSTICE HAS BEEN SERVED"

Many cars from Columbia went to Fulton carrying spectators to the hanging on December 18, 1936. A wet snow
fell throughout the night, making highway traffic treacherous,
and more than a half-dozen vehicles were seen in ditches between Columbia and Fulton. A hundred witnesses were not able
to attend because of the weather. Among those coming were Mrs.
Benjamin Booth and Mrs. Roger Wilson, widows of the two murdered officers.

The condemned man saw his lawyer George F. Hollis, that
night. Knowing death to be only a few hours away, McKeever told
his attorney he did not kill Sergeant Booth. Hollis spent several
hours with McKeever and returned home early in the morning.

Only a few feet from the gallows, guarded by Missouri Highway
patrolmen, McKeever ate a breakfast; consisting of two four-min-
ute eggs, toast, cornflakes, and coffee.

Although the scene was grim, no one showed any emotion.
About 200 witnesses stood in the enclosure and waited in the fall-
ing snow for McKeever, as he was taken from the city jail at 7 AM.
McKeever, wearing a dark blue suit and a gray cap, with a guard of
state troopers,

Colonel Casteel, head of the Missouri Highway Patrol, Sheriff Wells, and two priests, walked 200 feet across Fulton's main streets. About fifty highway patrolmen patrolled all roads to Fulton.

Officials had roped off several blocks adjoining the barn. State troopers formed a line along which the death party walked to the scaffold.[1]

McKeever ascended the thirteen steps that led to the scaffold floor. After he had mounted the scaffold, Casteel removed the cap from his head, and his hands were cuffed with steel.

Sheriff Wells asked McKeever if he had anything to say.

The gangster raised his head and looked directly at the crowd:

"Well, folks," he said, "you see me standing here. I forgive all who have done me any harm and hope that those I have harmed will forgive me, as I am about to leave this earth. That is all."

His legs and arms were strapped. The sheriff pulled a big black bag over McKeever's face, and Casteel put the noose around his neck. Sheriff Wells stepped back and pulled the lever at 7:33 AM. McKeever's body shot quickly through the scaffold floor opening; and, with a jerk of the rope and a twitch of the shoulders, the body straightened. Thirteen minutes later, two doctors from Fulton pronounced him dead.[2]

While the crowd dispersed, an ambulance was backed to the barn door, and McKeever's body was taken to an undertaker. It was prepared for shipment to his mother and wife in Burlington, Iowa. The mother had asked that the body be given to her for burial, but she did not have enough money for a funeral. It looked like the body might be turned over to the University of Missouri for medical research. However, Sheriff Wells was able to raise the money.

Alice Booth, widow of the slain trooper, told newspapermen, "I feel that justice has been served. He just the same as admitted his guilt," she said of McKeever's statement on the scaffold.

Mrs. Roger Wilson, whose husband was killed by Francis McNeiley, said she thought justice had been done to McKeever, but she believed that its ends would have been more fully met "if the other one was hanging there, too," her statement referring to McNeiley.

Casteel remarked McKeever made a statement admitting he had been at the crime scene, but said that he did not confess to the actual killing.

Of the hanging, Casteel said: "Sergeant Booth and Sheriff Wilson were exceptionally high type officers and were killed in the faithful performance of their duty. With the execution of McKeever, I feel that justice has been served."[3]

It was the last hanging in Missouri. The gangster was buried at the Burlington Memorial Park in Burlington, Iowa, on December 22, 1936.[4]

EPILOGUE

During November 1934, Richetti and Floyd were declared to be innocent of the charge they had murdered lawmen Benjamin Booth and Roger Wilson, near Columbia, Missouri, when Francis McNeiley admitted to the crime.[1]

The ex-convict, McNeiley, was a lucky man. After only fourteen years, he was paroled by Missouri Governor Phil Donnelly in 1947, even though he killed two policemen and the Minnesota storekeeper ,John Freund, as well as robbed banks and many other crimes.[2]

According to the autopsy report of Freund he would have died from a crushed skull caused by McNeiley, even if Eloy McKeever had not shot him. The Missouri Parole Board and Governor made no reference to Freund's murder.[3]

Even Lewis Means, the Chairman of the Missouri Board of Probation and Parole, who was the lawman who had arrested him for the murders, including the murder of a police officer from his own Missouri Highway Patrol, supported him.

McNeiley did not look like a murderer. After his parole, few people knew of his criminal history and thought of him as a nice

fellow who was a good business and family man. There were no
press reports of his parole or sentence commutation.[4]

On July 1, 1955, Iowa Parole Agent, F. D. Augustine, wrote to
Donald W. Bunker, Executive Secretary of the Missouri Board of
Probation and Parole, about McNeiley:

I am writing you again concerning the above named subject, who
has been on parole About seven years. He has made an excellent
parole and is a very fine citizen, associates with the best of people,
and gets along with everyone. He has a very good business in the
way of contracting and engineering. Makes a very good salary. Also
has a business of his own. Has a good home, paid for, on 42nd street
here. We certainly are proud of a fellow like Francis McNeiley when
we see all of the things he has accomplished in the last seven years.
Therefore, again I am recommending that he be discharged from
parole.[5]

On July 14, 1955, the Missouri Board of Probation and Parole
wrote to Missouri Governor
Donnelly about McNeiley:

There is herewith enclosed a recommendation from the
parole authority in the State of Iowa, recommending
that the subject, Francis McNeiley, be discharged from
parole.

McNeiley was sentenced on a plea of guilty to the crime
of murder in Boone County on June 18, 1935, for a crime
committed in April of 1933 /sic/, to a term of life.

McNeiley was from a middle class, but good family in
the southern tier of counties in Iowa, prior to his conflict
with the law. He had become associated with a band of
hardened criminals through the marriage of his sixteen-
year sister to one of the criminals, believing at the time he

was an honorable citizen and operator of an automobile repair business in Des Moines.

McNeiley, prior to his arrest, had broken with all his criminal associates, and had settled on a farm in southern Iowa, and was engaged in a normal life. Upon arrest, he promptly admitted the crime and assisted the officers in every way possible to solve the crime and to bring his accomplice to justice.

During the time he was an inmate of the institution here, he had a position of trust the entire period of his incarceration. /He/ was utilized by the institution officials to go to the other penal institutions at Tipton, Boonville, and Chillicothe, and, there, establish an excellent auditing and bookkeeping system for those institutions.

He was granted a parole on September 2, 1947, and transferred, under the Inter-State Compact to Des Moines, Iowa, under the supervision of Parole Officials of that state. All reports from over the period of seven years have been a succession of reports of excellent conduct and continuous progress. He has engaged in business and now owns an extremely profitable business, owns a $12,000 home, is married, and has a family. In view of this record and of the recommendation from the parole authorities of Iowa enclosed therewith, the Board recommends to the Governor that the subject's sentence be commuted as of the date of the Governor's approval.[6]

McNeiley returned to Iowa, married in 1948, and had four children. By all accounts, he was a good citizen the rest of his life. On September 29, 1955, the Governor commuted McNeiley's sentence, and his citizenship was restored one year later. He moved to St. Joseph, Missouri, in 1957, died there on April 13, 1991, and was buried in Memorial Park Cemetery in St. Joseph.[7]

Lewis Means continued in the Missouri Highway Patrol until December 1936, when Governor Lloyd C. Stark appointed him Missouri Adjutant General.[8]

On February 24, 1937, the Boone County, Missouri, Circuit Court refused to honor the Means' claim for a $400 reward offered by the county for the arrest and conviction of the the two lawmen's killers. The court ruled Means was acting in the line of duty as a major in the Missouri Highway Patrol, and the payment of the reward "would be against public policy."[9]

In the disastrous flood in southeast Missouri early in 1937, Means directed all federal and state agencies in relief and flood control.[10] He wrote an article entitled "Pretty Boy Floyd No. 2," about McKeever and McNeiley, for *Master Detective Magazine* in 1939.[11] Means was appointed Commanding General of the Missouri National Guard and became a Brigadier General. As General, he set up Fort Leonard Wood as a training camp.

During World War II, Means held several important jobs in the continental United States, such as Commander of the Northern California Anti-Sabotage Command, Head of the Northern Defense Area, Washington, Idaho, Oregon and Montana, and Chief of the Internal Security Division of the 9th Corps. In November 1942, he was put in charge of the Military Police on the Western Coast.

After the war, Means, became the Director of Security for the first United Nations meeting in San Francisco and protected President Truman when he visited the Conference.

When he had a heart attack in December 1945, he was released from active duty. Nine years later, Means became Chairman of the Missouri Parole Board. In 1958 he retired from that job and moved to Fayette, Missouri, where he died in June 1971.[12]

Merle Gill's Crime Lab went out of business in 1938. Police agencies no longer needed his help, as they had created or expanded their own crime labs during the 1930s.[13]

Ballistic tests about the killings of Missouri lawmen Booth and Forest and the Kansas City Massacre, one of the most important aspects of scientific police work, had not been done by the FBI Lab, but by Gill.[14] Gill made the important discovery that the machine gun that killed Kansas City mobster, John Lazia, on July 10, 1934, was used in the Kansas City Massacre. The FBI Lab later agreed.[15]

Gill also thought that the .45-caliber gun Pretty Boy Floyd had in his right hand at the time of his death was fired during the Kansas City Massacre, and that a shell from Floyd's gun was identical to a shell found at the scene of the massacre. This time, the FBI Lab disagreed, based on shell photographs.[16]

J. Edgar Hoover, upset over the disputes the FBI had with Gill, wrote, "Well, it serves us right for ever having dealt with Gill. I always opposed it & never approved the turning over of the evidence."[17] And again, "This sustains the opinion I had of Gill all along." It proves what a grievous error it was to turn over to him for examination of our evidence. We had a laboratory of our own & I never understand /sic/ why we dealt with this man."[18]

Hoover denounced Gill as having a "lack of ethics" and "certainly would never recommend this man with anything. Tell the Criminal Division that, in view of our experience with him, we could not conscientiously concur in any recommendation where his veracity or integrity is involved."[19] And finally, "We will have nothing to do with Gill."[20]

In 1939 Gill, like Means, wrote an article on the slayings of the two Missouri lawmen for *Master Detective Magazine*.[21] Gill died on December 25, 1960, in Los Angeles.[22]

Eloy McKeever entered the Minnesota State Penitentiary on January 22, 1935, with a life sentence. When he entered, a physical exam revealed a syphilitic condition, which was treated successfully.

For eighteen years, he worked as a maintenance mechanic in the prison twine shops. In March 1955, he earned minimum custody status and was assigned to the farm colony, where he worked as a groundkeeper, orderly, and all around utility man.

Reports on him were good, such as "Subject's work and conduct record have been very good." In another report, "For his age, he does a very good job, always polite and gets along well with people." Still another, "His institutional record has been excellent." He was somewhat more aggressive than the average lifer and not as institutionalized.

In 1956 and 1957, McKeever, dressed in civilian clothes, was in charge of the institutional twine exhibit at the Minnesota State Fair. It was an assignment which called for meeting the public and answering their questions concerning prison industries.[23]

On December 17, 1962, at the age of 66, McKeever was pardoned by the Minnesota Adult Corrections Commission. He had served twenty-five years, was said to be in good physical condition, and had average intelligence. They found him a home and work at Kern, California,[24] where he died on March 9, 1984.[25]

Lee Bostetter was confined to the St. Cloud Reformatory in Minnesota on June 11, 1935.

He was paroled on April 29, 1948, after serving twelve years. During his parole, he worked for a doctor in St. Cloud.[26] Bostetter married in 1950 and had six children.[27] His parole ended on September 30, 1956, and Minnesota Governor Orville Freeman restored his civil rights on October 8, 1956.[28] He was a longtime boiler engineer in Winona, Minnesota, and retired at the age of 62. Bostetter died in Winona on January 16, 2002, at the age of 92.[29]

According to Colonel B. Marvin Casteel, Director of the Missouri Highway Patrol, the McKeever gang was "one of the most troublesome robbery gangs in this part of the country."[30]

Members of the McKeever gang—George McKeever, Eloy McKeever, Lee Bostetter, and Francis McNeiley—killed two lawmen and a Minnesota store owner, were in a sensational car chase and gun fight, and stole at least $40,000 from about six banks. Today, that amounts to some $700,000.[31] George McKeever was also a member of the Reinhold Engel gang, "one of the cleverest and most efficient gangs of bank robbers."[32] Hundreds of burglaries were committed, numerous cars stolen, and many stores robbed. George McKeever and Francis McNeiley, alter egos of Pretty Boy Floyd and Adam Richetti, "contributed almost as much to the legends built up around the Southwest's 'phantom killer'" (i. e. Pretty Boy Floyd).[33]

After the "War on Crime" in the early 1930s, the FBI and law enforcement greatly increased in size and power from the excitement caused by the "Robin Hood" criminals and other bandits. As it did, the crime wave subsided.[34]

FOOTNOTES

Abbreviations
FBI SAC FBI Special Agent in Charge
FBI KCM File FBI Kansas City Massacre File

Introduction Footnotes

1. Missouri State Highway Patrol Website.
2. *Kansas City* MO *Star,* Jan. 3-5, 1932.
3. *Ibid.,* June 14-16, 1933.
4. *Ibid.,* June 17, 1933.
5. *Ibid.,* June 3, 1933.
6. *Ibid.,* June 14-16, 1933.
7. *Ibid.,* June 17, 1933.
8. Lee Louderback, **The Bad Ones: Gangsters of the '30s and Their Molls,** Greenwich, Conn., Fawett, 1968, 7-11.
9. John Toland, **The Dillinger Days,** New York, Random House, 1963, passim. Before 1935, the FBI was known as the Bureau of Investigation or the Division of Investigation until July 1935. To make it more simple, the term FBI is used at all times.

10. Michael Wallis, **Pretty Boy: The Life and Times of Charles Arthur Floyd,** New York, St. Martins Press, 1992, passim.

11. *Ibid.*

12. Bob L. Blackburn, "Law Enforcement in Transition: From Decentralized County Sheriffs to the Highway Patrol," **The Chronicles of Oklahoma,** 56, (Summer 1978, 200.

13. William Helmer with Rick Mattix, **Public Enemies: America's Criminal Past, 1919–1940,** New York, Checkmark Books, 1998, xi-xiv.

14. Toland, **The Dillinger Days,** New York, Random House, 1963, 36.

15. James E. Hamby, "The History of Firearms and Toolmark Identification ," 30th anniversary issue, v. 31, no. 3, Summer 1999, revised Apr. 2008.

16. G. Russell with William J. Helmer. **Dillinger: The Untold Story,** Blooming, Ind., Indiana University Press, 1994, 2.

17. *Ibid.*

18. Carl Sifakis, **The Encyclopia of American Crime,** New York, Smithmark Publishers, Inc., 1992, 345-347.

19. *Oelwein* IA *Register,* June 12, 1935.

20. *Ibid.*

21. FBI Identification Order No. 1194, June 22, 1933.

22. Gill, Crossroads.

23. Carl Sifakis, **The Encyclopedia of American Crime,** New York, Smithmark Publishers, Inc., 1992, passim.

PART 1.

Chapter 1 Footnotes
The Crossroads Murders

1. Merle A. Gill, "Death at the Crossroads," **Master Detective,** May 1939, v. 20, no. 3.
2. *Columbia* MO *Daily Tribune,* June 14, 1933.
3. 1900 U. S. Census
4. 1920 U. S. Census;
5. *Columbia* MO *Daily Tribune,* June 14, 15, 1933.
6. *Ibid.,* June 15, 1933.
7. *Shelbina* MO *Democrat,* June 21, 1933.
8. Trial of George McKeever, Callaway County, Missouri, Circuit Court, June 1935.

Chapter 2 Footnotes
"Let Us Hope the Hunt Will Go On Relentlessly"

1. *Columbia* MO *Daily Tribune,* June 15, 1933.
2. *Ibid.*
3. *Fayette* MO *Democrat-Leader,* June 12, 1971.
4. *Columbia* MO *Daily Tribune,* June 15, 1933.
5. *Ibid.,* June 16, 1933.
6. *Ibid.,* June 17, 1933.
7. *St. Louis* MO *Post-Dispatch,* June 19, 1933.

Chapter 3 Footnotes
The Kansas City Massacre

1. John Toland, **The Dillinger Days,** New York, Random House, 1963, 55-56.
2. Report, R. E. Vetterli, Kansas City, June 26, 1933, FBI KCM File.
3. *Ibid.*
4. Roger Unger, **The Union Station Massacre: The Original Sin of J. Edgar Hoover's FBI,**
5. Kansas City, MO., Andrew McMeel Publishing Company, 1997, 87.
6. Toland, **Dillinger Days,** 554-56;
7. Rept., W. F. Vetterli. Rept. W. Trainor, Kansas City, Oct. 19, 1934, FBI File.
8. Toland, **Dillinger Days, 55-56.**
9. William Helmer with Rick Mattix, **Public Enemies: America's Criminal Past, 1919- 1940,** New York, Checkmark Books, 1998, 185.
10. *Ibid.*
11. Byran Burrough, **Public Enemies: America's Greatest Crime Wave and the Birth of the FBI, 1933-34,** New York, The Penguin Press, 49-50.
12. *Ibid.*
13. *Ibid.*
14. *Ibid.*
15. *Ibid.*
16. *Ibid.*
17. *Ibid.*
18. *Ibid.*
19. *Ibid.*
20. Cowley to Hoover, Chicago, Oct. 1, 1933, KCM File.
21. *Ibid.*
22. Rept., W. F. Trainor.

23. *Ibid.*

24. Statement from Vivian Mathias, Sept. 30, 1934.FBI KCM File.

25. Cowley to Hoover, Chicago, Oct. 1, 1934. FBI KCM File.

26. Rept., W. F. Trainor.

27. *ibid.*

28. *Ibid.*

29. Merle Clayton, **Union Station Massacre; The Shootout That Started the FBI's War on Crime,** New York, leisure Books, 1975, 144.

30. *Ibid.*

Chapter 4 Footnotes
A Petty Thief

1. 1910 U. S. Census; Transcript of Proceedings, State of North Dakota vs. George McKeever, Richland County, N. D. Circuit Court, Nov. 19, 1934.
2. 1910 U. S. Census.
3. Sioux City, Iowa, Website.
4. 1920 U. S. Census; North Dakota vs. George McKeever.
5. U. S. Marine Crops Service Record of George McKeever.
6. North Dakota vs. George McKeever.
7. *Ibid.*
8. *Ibid.*
9. *9. Ibid.*
10. *10. Mason City* IA *Globe-Gazette,* June 11, 1928
11. 11. North Dakota vs. George McKeever.
12. Certificate of Death for George McKeever. Missouri Board of Health. Bureau of Vital Statistics.
13. North Dakota vs. George McKeever.

Chapter 5 Footnotes
"One of the Cleverest and Most Efficient Gangs
of Bank Robbers"

1. *Huron* SD *Evening Huronite,* May 15, 1932.
2. *Bismarck* ND *Tribune,* May 28, 1932.
3. *Richmond County* ND *Farmer-Globe,* June 19, 1930; *Bismarck* ND *Tribune,* May 30, 1930.
4. *Ibid.*
5. *Ibid.*
6. *Omaha* NE *World,* Aug. 15, 1930.
7. *Journal of Burnett* WI *County,* Feb. 15, 1931; *St. Paul* MN *Dispatch,* May 20, 1932.
8. *St. Paul* MN *Dispatch,* Jan 15, 1931; *Ibid.,* May 20, 1932.
9. *Atlantic* IA *News-Telegraph,* Mar. 10, 1931.
10. *Appleton* WI *Post-Crescent,* Mar. 24, 1931.
11. *Madison* WI *State Journal,* April 27, 1934.
12. *Huron* SD *Evening Huronite,* May 19, 1932.
13. *Bismarck* ND *Tribune,* May 28, 1932.

Chapter 6 Footnotes
"I Did Not Rob Any Banks"

1. Lewis M. Means and Vic Russell, "Snaring Missouri's Cop Slayers," **Dynamic Detective Monthly,** Oct. 1939, v. 6, no. 32.
2. *Columbian* MO *Missourian,* June 18, 1935.
3. 1920 U. S. Census; *Iowa Births and Christenings Index, 1857-1947. (Ancestry.com)*
4. Wayne County, Iowa, website.
5. *Hagerstown,* MD *Morning Herald,* June 27, 1935.
6. 1930 U. S. Census.
7. Means, "Cop Slayers."
8. *Ibid.;* 1920 U.S. Census.
9. **Rails of Memories,** Lucerne Centennial, 1887-1987. Lucerne, Mo., 1987; Means, "Cop Slayers."
10. Means, "Cop Slayers."
11. Trial of George McKeever, Callaway County, Missouri, Circuit Court, June 1935.
12. *Ibid.*
13. Means, "Cop Slayers.
14. *Mason City* IA *Globe-Gazette,* Oct. 28, Nov. 29, 1933.
15. Means, "Cop Slayers"
16. *Sioux City* IA *Journal,* Aug. 9, 10, 11, 1934; Dec. 18, 19, 1936.

Chapter 7 Footnotes
"Not One of the Weapons"

1. Merle A. Gill, "Death at the Crossroads," **Master Detective,** May 1939, v. 20, no. 3.
2. *Columbia* MO *Daily Tribune,* June 15, 1933.
3. Gill, "Crossroads."
4. 1900 U. S. Census; *Columbia* MO *Daily Tribune,* June 13, 1935; World War I Draft Registration of Merle A. Gill.
5. Gill, "Crossroads."
6. *Oelwein* IA *Daily Register,* June 13, 1935.
7. Gill, "Crossroads."
8. *Ibid.*
9. *Ibid.*

Chapter 8 Footnotes
"With Their Guns Spitting Bullets"

1. Deb Micklay, *Public Enemies in North Iowa,"* Aug. 30, 2009. (*Mason City* IA *Globegazette.com*)
2. *Cresco* IA *Plain Dealer,* Oct. 18, 1934.
3. *Hampton* IA *Chronicle,* Aug. 30, 1934; *Lime Springs* IA *Herald,* Jan. 17, 1935.
4. *Cresco* IA *Plain Dealer,* Oct. 18, 1934.
5. *Ibid.*
6. *Ibid.*
7. *Oelwein* IA *Daily Register,* Oct. 12, 1934.
8. *Cresco* IA *Plain Dealer,* Oct. 18, 1934.
9. *Ibid.*

Chapter 9 Footnotes
Who Was Eddie Bennett?

1. Lewis M. Means and Vic Russell, *"Snaring Missouri's Cop Slayers,"* **Dynamic Detective,** Oct. 1939, v. 1, no. 39.
2. *Ibid.*
3. *Ibid.*
4. *Ibid.*
5. *Ibid.*

Chapter 10 Footnotes
"One of the Most Fiendish Crimes"

1. *Mason City* IA *Globe-Gazette,* Oct. 22, 1934.
2. *Ibid.*
3. *Ibid.*
4. Minnesota Parole Report of Eloy McKeever.
5. *Mason City* IA *Globe-Gazette,* Oct. 22, 1934.
6. *Albert Lee* MN *Evening Tribune,* Oct. 22, 1934.
7. *Mason City* IA *Globe-Gazette,* Oct. 22, 1934.
8. *Albert Lee* MN *Evening Tribune,* Oct. 22, `2934.
9. *Mason City* IA *Globe-Gazette,* Oct. 22, 1934.
10. *Mason City* IA *Globe-Gazette,* Oct. 24, 1934; Minnesota Parole Report of Eloy McKeever.
11. *Mason City* IA *Globe-Gazette,* Oct. 24, 1934.
12. *Mason City* IA *Globe-Gazette,* Oct. 27, 1934.
13. Lewis M. Means and Vic Russell, *"Snaring Missouri's Cop Slayers,"* **Dynamic Detective,** Oct. 1939, v. 6., no. 12.

Chapter 11 Footnotes
"I Do Not Believe This is the Time to Compromise with
Criminals"

1. *Richmond County* ND *Farmer-Globe,* Nov. 13, 1934.
2. *Ibid.*
3. *Ibid.*
4. *Ibid.,* Nov. 20, 1934.
5. *Ibid.*
6. *Ibid.*
7. *Ibid.*
8. *Ibid.*

PART 2

Chapter 12 Footnotes
"The Big Break"

1. Lewis M. Means and Vic Russell, *"Snaring Missouri's Cop Slayers,"* **Dynamic Detective,** Oct. 1939, v. 6, no. 32
2. *Ibid.*
3. *Ibid.*
4. *Ibid.*
5. *Ibid.*
6. *Ibid.*

Chapter 13 Footnotes
"I See You Have Quite a Store Here"

1. *Ida County* IA *Pioneer,* Dec. 27, 1934.
2. *Jefferson* MO *Post Tribune,* Dec. 28, 1934.

Chapter 14 Footnotes
"I Don't Even Know What You are Talking About"

1. *Austin* MN *Daily Herald,* Dec. 29, 1934.
2. *Ibid.*
3. *Ibid.,* Jan. 2, 1935.
4. *Ibid.,* Jan. 4, 1935.
5. *Moorhead* MN *Daily News,* Jan. 4, 1935.
6. *Austin* MN *Daily Herald,* Jan. 7, 1935.
7. *Ibid.,* Jan. 11, 1935.

Chapter 15 Footnotes
"My God, You Don't Think I intended to Kill that Man?"

1. *Austin* MN *Daily Herald,* Jan. 18, 1935.
2. *Ibid.*
3. *Ibid.*
4. *Ibid.*
5. *Ibid.*
6. *Albert Lee* MN *Evening Journal,* Jan. 21, 1935.
7. *Ibid.*
8. *Ibid.*
9. *Ibid.*
10. *Austin* MN *Daily Herald,* Jan. 21, 1935.
11. *Ibid.*
12. *Ibid.,* Jan. 22, 1935.

Chapter 16 Footnotes
Ten More Years

1. *Austin* MN *Daily Herald,* Mar. 13, 1935.
2. *Ibid.,* Mar. 17, 1935.
3. *Ibid.,* Mar. 18, 1935.
4. *Mason City* IA *Globe-Gazette,* Apr. 10, 1935.

Chapter 17 Footnotes
"I am Ready to Pay"

1. *Muskogee* OK *Daily Phoenix,* Nov. 28, 1934.
2. *Mason City* IA *Globe-Gazette,* Jan. 3, 1935.
3. *Moberly* IA *Monitor-Index,* Dec. 28, 1934.
4. *Jefferson City* MO *Post-Tribune,* Feb. 4, 1935.
5. *Austin* MN *Daily Herald,* Jan. 15, 1935.
6. *Ibid.,* Jan. 21, 1935.
7. *Ibid.,* Jan. 15, 1935.
8. *Mason City* IA *Globe-Gazette,* Jan. 26, 1935.
9. *Jefferson City* MO *Post-Tribune,* Feb. 4, 1935.
10. *Joplin* MO *Globe,* Mar. 14, 1935.
11. "Hard Work, Not Magic Solves Murder Case," Wilmington DE *Sunday Star,* Sept. 1, 1935.
12. *Ibid.*
13. Merle A. Gill, *Death at the Crossroads,* **Master Detective,** May 1939, v. 20, no. 3.

Chapter 18 Footnotes
"An Endeavor to Prejudice The Jurors and Spectators"

1. *Fulton Missouri Telegraph,* June 13, 1935.
2. *Fulton* MO *Daily Sun-Gazette,* June 12, 1935.

Chapter 19 Footnotes
"This is a Highway Patrol Case"

1. *Fulton Missouri Telegraph,* June 13, 1935.
2. *Ibid.*
3. *Ibid.*
4. *Ibid.*
5. *Ibid.*
6. *Ibid.*
7. *Fulton* MO *Daily Sun-Gazette,* June 12, 1935.
8. *Ibid.*
9. *Ibid.*
10. *Ibid.*
11. *Ibid.*

Chapter 20 Footnotes
"I Expect to Get The Supreme Penalty"

1. *Fulton* MO *Daily Sun-Gazette,* June 15, 1935.
2. *Ibid.*

Chapter 21 Footnotes
"We Access the Punishment at Death"

1. Ful*lton* MO *Daily Sun-Gazette,* June 14, 1935.
2. *Ibid.*
3. *Ibid.*
4. *Columbia* MO *Tribune,* June 17, 1935.
5. *Columbia* MO *Missourian,* June 17, 1935.
6. *Kansas City* MO Star, June 16, 1935.
7. *Fulton* MO *Sun-Gazette,* June 17, 1935.
8. *Moberly* MO *Monitor-Index,* June 17, 1935.
9. *Columbia* MO *Daily Tribune,* June 17, 1935.
10. *Columbia* MO *Missourian,* June 18, 1935.
11. *Ibid.*
12. *Ibid.*
13. *Jefferson City* MO *Post-Tribune,* June 19, 1935.

Chapter 22 Footnotes
"The Bloodiest Forty-Seven Acres in America"

1. Donald Schroeger, *The Course of Corrections in Missouri,* in
   Official Manual, Missouri, 1983-1984. (Jefferson, Office
   of Missouri Secretary of State, 1983), 1-23; *"MSP Historical
   Information,"* **The Jefftown Journal, Historical Ed.,** (Summer
   1972).

Chapter 23 Footnotes
"McKeever Must Pay for Murder With His Life"

1. Jamie Pamela Rasmussen, **The Missouri State Penitentiary,** Columbia, Mo., University of Missouri Press, 2012, 57-58.
2. *Columbia* MO *Missourian,* June 18, 1935.
3. *Moberly* MO *Monitor-Index,* July 13, 1935.
4. *Monitor* MO *Index and Democrat,* Aug. 19, 1935.
5. *Massillon* OH *Evening Independent,* Sept. 26, 1935.
6. *Jefferson City* MO *Post-Telegraph,* Nov. 17, 1935.
7. *Ibid.*
8. *Moberly* MO *Monitor-Index,* Dec. 16, 1936.

Chapter 24 Footnotes
"Reconciled to His Fate"

1. *Jefferson City* MO *Post-Tribune,* Dec. 9, 1936.
2. *Ibid.,* Dec. 14, 1936.
3. *Columbia* MO *Daily Tribune,* Dec. 13, 1936.
4. *Ibid.,* Dec. 14, 1936.
5. *Ibid.,* Dec. 15, 1936.
6. *Ibid.,* Dec. 16, 1936.
7. *Moberly* MO *Monitor-Index,* Dec. 16, 1936.
8. *Jefferson City* MO *Post-Tribune,* Dec. 16, 1936.
9. *Chester* PA *Times,* Dec. 17, 1936.
10. *Columbia* MO *Daily Tribune,* Dec. 14, 15, 1936.
11. *Ibid.,* Dec. 18, 1936.

Chapter 25 Footnotes
"I Feel Justice Had Been Done"

1. *Columbia* MO *Daily Tribune,* Dec. 18, 1936.
2. *Ibid.*
3. *Ibid.*
4. Findagrave.com

Epilogue Footnotes

1. *Muskogee* OK *Daily Phoenix,* Nov. 28, 1934.
2. Commutation of the sentence of Francis McNeiley by Missouri Governor Phil M. Donnelly, Sept. 29, 1955.
3. Minnesota Parole Report of Eloy McKeever..
4. Commutation of Francis McNeiley.
5. *Ibid.*
6. Ibid.
7. *St. Joseph* MO *News Press/Gazette,* April 14, 1991.
8. *Fayette* MO *Democrat-Leader,* June 12, 1971.
9. *Mason City* IA *Globe-Gazette,* Feb. 25, 1937.
10. *Fayette* MO *Democrat-Leader,* June 12, 1971.
11. Lewis M. Means and Vic Russell, "Snaring Missouri's Cop Slayers," **Dynamic Detective,** Oct. 1939, v. 1, no. 39..
12. *Fayette* MO *Democrat-Leader,* June 12, 1971.
13. *Joplin* MO *Globe,* Sept. 10, 1938.
14. Merle Gill, "Death at the Crossroads," **Master Detective,** May 1939, v.20, no. 5,.
15. Letter, Director to Special-Agent-in-Charge (SAC), Kansas City, Aug. 7, 1934. FBI KCM File.
16. Letter, SAC, Kansas City, to Director, Aug. 7, May 9, 1935. FBI KCM File.
17. Memorandum for the Director from E. A. Tamm,, Nov. 7, 1934. FBI KCM File.
18. *Ibid.,* Feb. 26, 1935. FBI KCM File.
19. Letter, SAC, Kansas City, to Director, Nov. 6, 1934. FBI KCM File.
20. *Ibid.*
21. Gill, "Death at the Crossroads."
22. California Death Index, 1940-1997.
23. Minnesota Parole Record of Eloy McKeever.
24. *Ibid.*

25. Social Security Death Index; California Death Index, 1940-1997.

26. Minnesota Parole Record of Lee Bostetter.

27. *Winona* MN *Daily News,* Jan. 18, 2002.

28. Minnesota Parole Record of Lee Bostetter.

29. *Winona* MN *Daily News,* Jan. 18, 2002.

30. *Austin* MN *Daily Register,* Dec. 29, 1934.

31. Lewis M. Means and Vic Russell, *"Snaring Missouri's Cop Slayers,"* **Dynamic Detective,** Oct. 1939, v. 1, no. 39.

32. *Huron* SD *Evening Huronite,* May 15, 1932.

33. *Oelwein* IA *Daily Register,* June 12, 1935.

34. Carl Sifakis, **The Encyclopedia of American Crime,** New York, Smithmark Publishers, Inc., 1992, 345-347.

SELECT BIBLIOGRAPHY

BOOKS

Burrough, Brian. **Public Enemies: America's Greatest Crime Wave and the Birth of the FBI.** New York, The Penguin Press, 2004.

Clayton, Merle. **Union Station Massacre: The Shootout That Started the FBI's War on Crime,** New York, Leisure Books, 1973.

King, Jeffery S. **The Life and Death of Pretty Boy Floyd.** Kent, Ohio, Kent State university Press, 1998.

Toland, John. **The Dillinger Days.** New York, Random House, 1963.

Unger, Robert. **The Union Station Massacre: The Original Sin of Hoover's FBI.** Kansas City, Mo., Andrews, McNeel, 1997.

Wallis, Michael. **Pretty Boy: The Life and Times of Charles Arthur Floyd.** New York, St. Martin's Press, 1992.

ARTICLES

Gill, Merle A. *"Death at the Crossroads,"* **Master Detective,** May 1939, v. 20, no. 3.

King, Jeffery S., *"Pretty Boy Floyd's Double,"* **Informer: The History of American Crime and Law Enforcement,** Nov. 2014.

Means, Lewis M., and Vic Russell, *"Snaring Missouri's Cop Slayers,"* **Dynamic Detective,** Oct. 1939, v.6, no. 32.

NEWSPAPERS

Albert Lee MN *Evening Tribune*
Austin MN *Daily Herald*
Columbia MO *Daily Tribune*
Columbian MO *Missourian*
Fulton MO *Daily Sun-Gazette*
Fulton MO *Missouri Telegraph*
Kansas City MO *Star*
Mason City IA *Globe-Gazette*
Moberly MO Monitor-Index
New York Times
Richmond County ND *Farmer-Gazette*
St. Louis MO *Post-Dispatch*
Tulsa OK *Daily World*

PRIMARY SOURCES

Ancestry.com
Court Records
FBI Kansas City Massacre File
Parole Records
Prison records
U. S. Census
U. S. Marine Corps Service. Record of George McKeever

INDEX

Page numbers followed by "*f*" indicate figures/pictures.

CPSIA information can be obtained
at www.ICGtesting.com
Printed in the USA
LVHW080152151120
671495LV00005B/531